exploring

HEAVENLY PLACES

DISCERNMENT ENCYCLOPEDIA FOR GOD'S SPIRITUAL CREATION

VOLUME 7

By

Paul L Cox

Barbara Kain Parker

EXPLORING HEAVENLY PLACES, VOLUME 7
Discernment Encyclopedia for God's Spiritual Creation

By Paul L Cox and Barbara Kain Parker

Aslan's Place Publications
9315 Sagebrush Street
Apple Valley, CA 92308
760-810-0990
www.aslansplace.com

Unless otherwise indicated, scriptures are taken from the:
New King James Version (NKJV): New King James Version®. Copyright © 1982 by Thomas Nelson. Used by permission. All rights reserved.

Scripture taken from HOLY BIBLE, NEW INTERNATIOANL VERSION ®. Copyright © 1973, 1978, 1984 by International Bible Society. Used by permission of Zondervan. All rights reserved.

Copyright 2017, by Paul L Cox and Barbara Kain Parker
All rights reserved.
Editor: Barbara Kain Parker
Illustrations: Jana Green
Cover Design: Brodie Schmidtke
ISBN # 978-1-5136-1988-0
Printed in the United States of America

ACKNOWLEDGEMENTS

With gratitude we would like to acknowledge the contributions of some special friends: Jana Green, Rob Gross, Larry Pearson, Tobias Renken, and Brodie Schmidtke. All of these have played important roles in our journeys of exploration to define and discern God's amazing creations in the heavenly places.

Jana Green, a gifted artist, prayer minister, prophetic intercessor is the illustrator for the discernment drawings in this book. She has also shared her person discernment and has provided the discernment mapping in Appendix 1. Jana's website is http://www.signsandwondersstudio.com

Rob Gross, the pastor of Mountain View Community Church in Kanahoe, Hawaii, has contributed the Foreword as well as his discernment observations. Rob is also the co-author of *Exploring Heavenly Places, Volume 2* and the author of *Volume 6*.

Tobias Renken and Larry Pearson have shared their personal discernment observations. Tobias is a long-time friend and prophetic intercessor for Aslan's Place who lives in Germany and participates regularly in the webinars. Larry is co-founder of Lion Sword Solutions and many of his prophetic words can be found throughout the *Exploring Heavenly Places* series. His website is http://lionsword.ca

Brodie Schmidtke, who originally designed the cover for *Volume 1*, adapts it for each book in the series.

Thanks to all!
Paul Cox and Barbara Parker

TABLE OF CONTENTS

FOREWORD

Jesus once made a perplexing statement, *"You therefore must be perfect, as your Heavenly Father is perfect."* [1] Just eleven words, but what was He saying? I believe that He was referring to the point in time when the Church would become mature like His Father. This raises another question, "What is maturity?" *Webster's Dictionary* defines it as, 'the condition of being fully developed'. The Greek word for mature (or perfect) is the adjective, *teleios*, derived from the word *telos*, meaning 'consummated goal'. In other words, maturity is the result of going through the necessary stages to reach the end goal; it's fulfilling the necessary process of one's spiritual journey. The root *tel* means 'reaching the end'; it is like a pirate's telescope, extending out one stage at a time to achieve full strength capacity and effectiveness. A biblical snapshot of what such strength and effectiveness looks like is the account of Jesus healing a man instantly—one who had been paralyzed for 38 years:

> *Afterward Jesus returned to Jerusalem for one of the Jewish holy days. Inside the city, near the Sheep Gate, was the pool of Bethesda, with five covered porches. Crowds of sick people—blind, lame, or paralyzed—lay on the porches. One of the men lying there had been sick for thirty-eight years. When Jesus saw him and knew he had been ill for a long time, he asked him, "Would you like to get well?" "I can't, sir," the sick man said, "for I have no one to put me into the pool when the water bubbles up. Someone else always gets there ahead of me." Jesus told him, "Stand up, pick up your mat, and walk!" Instantly, the man was healed! He rolled up his sleeping mat and began walking! But this miracle happened on the Sabbath, so the Jewish leaders objected. They said to the man who was cured, "You can't work on the Sabbath! The law doesn't allow you to carry that sleeping mat!" So Jesus explained, "I tell you the truth, the Son can do nothing by himself. He does only what he sees the Father doing. Whatever the Father does, the Son also does. For the Father loves the Son and shows him everything he is doing. In fact, the Father will show him how to do even greater works than healing this man. Then you will truly be astonished.* [2]

Among all who had gathered at the pool of Bethesda that day why did Jesus pick this man? His words were very clear—He only did what he saw His Father doing, and wanted to join into that process. But what does that have to do with our maturity, and why does God want us to be perfect? Simple—it's so we will recognize, like Jesus did, our Father' intentions so we can cooperate with Him to achieve His purposes. As we become mature sons and daughters we will know what the Father is doing, and we will be able to perform the greater works He promised.[3] Such Christian maturity is tied to the spiritual gift of discernment:

> For the earnest expectation of the creation eagerly waits for the revealing of the sons of God.[4]

> But solid food is for the mature, who because of practice have their senses trained to discern good and evil.[5]

Exploring Heavenly Places, Volume 7: Discernment Encyclopedia for God's Spiritual Creation is a 'must-have' book because it clearly explains how we can understand what the Father is initiating in the heavenly places through discernment of His spiritual reality. I cannot think of a better resource that you can acquire to help you learn how to partner with the Father and release the kingdom of God wherever you are. I believe that Paul L. Cox and Barbara Kain Parker have compiled a book, complete with illustrations by Jana Green, that one day will be considered a classic.

Rob Gross
Mountain View Community Church

[1] Matthew 5:48 ESV

[2] John 5:1-3, 5-10, 19-20 NLT

[3] John 14:12

[4] Romans 8:19

[5] Hebrews 5:14

INTRODUCTION

We write of *Exploring Heavenly Places*, but what does that actually mean? A quick look at a few dictionary definitions[1] of 'explore' are quite illuminating as we consider the word in the context of the God's unseen creation. To explore is to investigate, study, or analyze; to travel in or through an unfamiliar country or area in order to learn about or familiarize oneself with it; to search for resources; to inquire into or discuss an issue in detail, examining or evaluating options or possibilities; and to examine by touch. By default, exploration has to do with searching out the unknown, and what can be more unfamiliar from our physical perspective than the mysteries of God that exist in His heavenly places?

Our exploration of heavenly places is through discernment, which is understanding gained through the use of our five senses. Diagrams, or discernment maps, are included in Section 2, which show where certain individuals feel things on their heads. But, please remember that nothing is always, and depending on individual gifts the way one person discerns may not be identical to another, and a sensation may occur anywhere on one's body. In fact, discernment may not be a feeling at all, but could be a sight, sound, smell, or taste that alerts an individual to manifestations in heavenly places.

> *But solid food belongs to those who are of full age, that is, those who by reason of use have their **senses** exercised to discern both good and evil.*[2]

Rob Gross offers a good analogy: In flight school aspiring pilots are taught in a flight simulator to take note of what is going on with their bodies in an oxygen-deprived environment. They are trained to be aware of what is going on with their bodies in the event that something might occur on an actual flight. Similarly, the Lord trains us to discern or sense good and evil on our bodies so that we are aware of what is going on in the spiritual realm and can respond to what the Father is doing.

It should be noted that there is plenty of biblical evidence to support discernment with all five senses, only a few of which can be offered here:[3]

> Then the Lord said to Moses, "Stretch out your hand toward heaven, that there may be darkness over the land of Egypt, darkness which may even be **felt**."[4]

> Is there injustice on my tongue? Cannot my **taste** discern the unsavory?[5]

> And walk in love, as Christ also has loved us and given Himself for us, an offering and a sacrifice to God for a sweet-**smelling** aroma.[6]

> And I **heard** a man's voice between the banks of the Ulai, who called, and said, "Gabriel, make this man understand the vision."[7]

> …the heavens were opened and I **saw** visions of God.[8]

> Immediately the fountain of her blood was dried up, and she **felt** in her body that she was healed of the affliction.[9]

> So I went to the angel and said to him, "Give me the little book." And he said to me, "Take and eat it; and it will make your stomach bitter, but it will be as sweet as honey in your **mouth**."[10]

> Indeed I have all and abound. I am full, having received from Epaphroditus the things sent from you, a sweet-**smelling** aroma, an acceptable sacrifice, well pleasing to God.[11]

> I was in the Spirit on the Lord's Day, and I heard behind me a loud voice, as of a trumpet…[12]

> But he, being full of the Holy Spirit, gazed into heaven and saw the glory of God, and Jesus standing at the right hand of God, and said, "Look! I see the heavens opened and the Son of Man standing at the right hand of God!"[13]

Then he fell to the ground, and heard a voice saying to him, "Saul, Saul, why are you persecuting Me?"…And the men who journeyed with him stood speechless, hearing a voice but seeing no one.[14]

As we considered our next topic in this series, we realized that it might be wise to develop a reference manual since many of our readers may be new to the concept of discerning that which we do not see. Others may be familiar with the common belief among many Christians that every scriptural being is simply a different kind of angel; but we identify angels as angels, cherubs as cherubs, elders as elders, powers as powers, and so on down the list.

Additionally, it is important to realize that every created thing in the heavenly places is alive; nothing is dead or inanimate as it is on earth, so what we might consider inanimate here is very different there.

Our prayer for our readers is the same as the Apostle Paul offered for the Philippians:

And this I pray, that your love may abound still more and more in knowledge and all discernment, that you may approve the things that are excellent, that you may be sincere and without offense till the day of Christ, being filled with the fruits of righteousness which are by Jesus Christ, to the glory and praise of God.[15]

[1] http://www.merriam-webster.com/dictionary/explore
http://www.oxforddictionaries.com/us/definition/american_english/explore

[2] Hebrews 5:14

[3] Ephesians 1:20-21, Philippians 2:9-10, 2 Thessalonians 1:7, Hebrews 1 & 2, John 1:1-3; Psalm 104:4

[4] Exodus 10:21

[5] Job 6:30

[6] Ephesians 5:2

[7] Daniel 8:16

[8] Ezekiel 1:1

[9] Mark 5:29

[10] Revelation 10:9

[11] Ephesians 4:18

[12] Revelation 1:10

[13] Acts 7:55-56

[14] Acts 9:4, 7

[15] Philippians 1:9-11

USING THIS GUIDE

We have categorized each entry as God, Being, Entity, or Place whenever possible, with a few entries sharing more than one category. Except for 'Evil Default', which describes the discernment of evil, only righteous entries are included in the guide. Appendix 2 offers additional insights into discerning evil, objects, and other things that are not listed here.

Categories are not absolute but are offered as a way to help increase understanding, and are differentiated as:

1. **God** is the Creator of all that exists. Known by many names and descriptions throughout the Bible, He has allowed us to begin to discern Him in a few of His various roles.

2. **Beings** have self-determination and move about; they can process information and act on it.

3. **Entities** are more static and function according to a prescribed purpose. Sometimes they may be used or manipulated by a being; they may respond to a command, as when Jesus spoke to the fig tree; [1] or they may even move or speak, as do elements of creation that declare the glory of God. [2] A good example in the physical realm would be a tree—alive and growing, roots digging down for nourishment while branches reach up toward the sun, functioning according to God's perfect design.

4. **Places** are dimensional locations. They are synonymous with domains or realms, which could compare to such physical examples as houses, cities, countries, oceans, etc. (Note: domains may be either beings or places.)

Please keep in mind the following:

1. The Bible is the final source of truth and we do not base our discernment in the heavenly places on extra-biblical material, and everything we discern must be tested against the Bible.

2. Christ is above all of creation. Every created thing we discern

is subject to Him.[3]

3. Operating through progressive revelation about what the Bible says, our views may change as new understanding is developed.

4. Discernment is not ability, but is a spiritual gift from God. We cannot truthfully perceive the supernatural on our own.

Helpful hints for using this book:

1. Whenever possible, each entry is described under headings of category, history, definition, key scriptures, characteristics, functions, observations, and discernment. Not all categories are available for every entry.

2. The number in parenthesis following an entry indicates where it will be found on the discernment map.

3. The discernment of Paul (and others) has expanded to the point that several different things may be felt on the same spot and/or in the same way, in which case he mentions the specific word(s) (i.e. golden pipes) and gets a 'hit' (increased pressure) that allows him to know which it is.

4. When left or right is indicated: The right and left can indicate the mother's side (left) or the father's side (right). Some believe left indicates what you are born with and right indicates what you should have faith for.

5. Regarding listings for spiritual gifts, each seems to have both a male and female portion.

6. Please remember that your own discernment may or may not be the same as that which is described.

---

[1] Mark 11

[2] Psalm 19:1-4

[3] John 1:3; Colossians 1:16

DISCERNMENT GUIDE

ANCIENT OF DAYS (1)
Category: God

History: First discerned, 2009

Definition: Hebrew: *attîq,* 'ancient' (of days), used only in regard to God in Daniel 7[1]

Key Scriptures: Daniel 7:9, 13, 22

Characteristics: Often discerned in the context of being taken into the Ancient of Days court

Observations:
- Implies rule, judgment, power, imparts information
- Has to do with ruling and reigning, and unity with God

Discernment:
- Paul: Feels an anointing all over the top of the head

- Jana: Sees ancient books opened

- Rob: Feels a sensation over the entire head from front to back

- Larry: See a book; have a sense of something ancient

- Tobias: Feels power upper, back of head, as if big electrical cable plugged in with strong current; sees what is occurring in the court; an observer and a participant; have to achieve a certain degree of unity and surrender with the Lord

ANGEL (2)—SEE ALSO: ANGEL OF THE LORD, BREAKTHROUGH ANGEL, RAINBOW ANGEL, EMERALD ANGEL, TONGUES OF ANGELS, ARCHANGEL, MICHAEL, GABRIEL
Category: Being

History: First discerned, 1992

Definition: Hebrew: *malak,* 'angel'; Greek: *aggelos,* 'angel', 'messenger'; generally a (supernatural) messenger from God, an angel conveying news or behests from God to men[2]

Key Scriptures: Due to extensive number of scriptures regarding angels, references are sorted topically

Characteristics:

- More than 300 direct references in angels in the Bible
- Organized and numbered by thousands and legions, innumerable, militaristic (Hebrews 12:22, Revelation 5:11, Matthew 26:53, Revelation 12:7-9)
- Masculine or feminine in nature (Zechariah 5:9)
- Created before the earth (Psalm 104:1-5)
- Created for us (Hebrews 1:14)
- Heavenly beings (Luke 2: 13-15, 22:43; Matthew 18:10, 22:30, 24:36, 22:43)
- Belong to God (Luke 12:8-9, 15:10; Matthew 16:27, 24:31)
- Inferior to Jesus (Hebrews 1:4,5,8; Psalm 104:4)
- Spirit beings (Hebrews 1:14)
- Limited in knowledge (Matthew 24:36)
- Like the wind or fire (Psalm 104:4; Hebrews 1:7; Revelation 10:1, 14:18)
- Sometimes may be seen, have freedom to appear (1 Kings 6:16-17, Luke 1:11-13, 26-29))
- Make specific sounds (Revelation 10:3, 1 Corinthians 13: 13; Luke 2:13-14; Revelation 5:13)
- Curious (1 Peter 1:12)
- Need assistance at times (Daniel 10:13)
- Expend energy (Revelation 12:7)
- Appear youthful (Mark 16:15)
- Powerful (2 Peter 2:11; Acts 12:7-11; Matthew 28:2; Mark16:3-5)
- Governed by God (Genesis 18:2)
- Walk like man (Genesis 18:2, 18:16, 19:1)
- Immortal (Mark 12:25; Luke 20:34-36)
- Truthful (Revelation 19:9; Galatians 3:19)
- Located in many places in the tabernacle

Functions:

- Deliver messages and special instructions (Psalm 103:20; Luke

1, 2; Daniel 8, 12:4, Isaiah 44:26, Acts 8:26-27)

- Put laws into effect (Acts 7:53; Galatians 3:19)
- Warriors (2 Kings 2:11; Psalm 34:7, 78:49, 103:19-20; Revelation 9:14-15, 15:1, 15:6, 20:1-3)
- Protect (Psalm 34:7; Daniel 6:19-22)
- Rescue (Daniel 3:24-25; Acts 12:11; Genesis 19:15-17, 16:7-9; Exodus 23:20-21; Numbers 22:22-35; 2 Kings 1:15; Matthew 2:13, 26:53; Acts 10:3-33; Luke 22:43)
- Prophesy, teach, and encourage (Luke 1:11-13, 2:9-12; Matthew 28:1-7; Acts 27:20-26; Revelation 14:6-7)
- Visit us (Hebrews 13:2)
- Serve God (Revelation 19:10, 22:8-9)
- Worship (Matthew 18:10, Psalm 103:20-22, 148:1-3; Hebrews 1:6)
- Carry us up to heaven (Luke 16:22)
- Punish God's enemies (Acts 12:23; Genesis 19:1,12-13)
- Control elements of nature (Revelation 7:1, 16:8-9)
- Minister, give direction (Revelation 10:1-10)
- Travel through portals (Genesis 28:12-13, John 1:51)
- Appear in dreams (Genesis 31:10-13; Matthew 1:20-25, 2:13)
- Rejoice (Luke 15:10)
- Observe us (1 Corinthians 4:9, 11:10; 1 Timothy 3:16, 5:21; Luke 12:8-9)
- Put God's seal on foreheads (Revelation 7:3-4)
- Guard us (Psalm 91:11-12; Matthew 18:10; Acts 12:13-16)
- Carry out great tasks (Hebrews 1:7, 14)
- See Jesus (1 Timothy 3:16)

Observations:

- When people die, they do not become angels
- Angels do not dwell inside of people
- Angels do not earn their wings
- No evidence God is creating more angels

- Angels do not marry (Matthew 22:30)

- Angels are not omnipresent (Daniel 9:21-23)

- Satan tried to persuade Jesus to ask help from angels (Matthew 4:6)

- Angels do not mediate (Revelation 1:1, 22:6, 22:16; 1 Timothy 2:5)

- We must not let angels replace or come before God in our lives (Psalm 42:1; Colossians 2:18; Romans 1:25; Revelation 19:10, 22:8-9, Galatians 1:8)

- Do not worship or pray to angels (Revelation 22:8-9)

- No example in scripture of people asking God to send angels or of people summoning and commanding angels

- Although there are scriptural examples of talking with angels (i.e. Mary), extreme caution should be used; it is probably not advisable to talk to angels unless you have a very clear sense from the Lord

- We do not believe the term 'angels' is inclusive of all righteous spiritual beings

Discernment: Often felt in a specific place on the head; may also feel tingling, warmth, or a heaviness in the air with a hand; various angels may be discerned differently according to name or function

- Paul: Left middle of head about 2 inches from left side

- Jana: Varies with type of angel: message angel feels as if she is inside with pressure on right, top of head

- Rob: Left side of head

- Larry: Senses them in the room; can vary with different types; mostly by a knowing

- Tobias: Sees them

ANGEL OF THE LORD (3)—SEE ALSO: ANGEL

Category: Being

History: First discerned, early 2000s, when the furnace appeared

Definition: *NIV Study Bible* note on Genesis 16:8: Since the angel of the Lord speaks for God in the first person (v.10) and Hagar is said to name the Lord who spoke to her: 'You are the God who sees me' (v.13), the angel appears to be both distinguished from the Lord (in that he is called 'messenger'-the Hebrew for 'angel' means messenger') and identified with him. Traditional interpretation has held this 'angel' was a pre-incarnate manifestation of Christ as God's Messenger-Servant. It may be, however, that, as the Lord's personal messenger who represented him and bore his credentials, the angel could speak on behalf of (and so be identified with) the One who sent him. Whether this 'angel' was the second person of the Trinity remains therefore uncertain.

Key Scriptures: Genesis 16:7-13, 18:22-33, 31:11-13, 22:11-18, 32:24-32, 48:15-16 (KJV); Exodus 3:2,4,6-8,14, 13:21-22, 14-19, 32:34 –33:3,14-17; Joshua 5:13-15; Judges 2:1, 6:11-13, 13:1-21; 2 Samuel 24:15-17: 1 Chronicles 21:1, 14:15, 21:18, 24-29; 2 Kings 19:35; Psalm 34; Isaiah 37:36; Zechariah 1:12-13, 3:1-7; Matt 24:44-51, 25:32-42, 26:28, 28:19-20; Luke 4:16-19; John 1:14,18, 9:35-38, 16:1-4, 17:6; Acts 12:21-23; Romans 11:25-26, 15:18-19; Ephesians 1:7; Colossians 2:9; Hebrews 2:14-15,13:5, 9:15; I John 2:1-2; Revelation 5:5, 6:1-17

Characteristics: Located at the Bronze Altar near the entrance to the Tabernacle; may be personal attendant(s) of the Lord (see Genesis 18)

Functions: Revelation; commissioning; deliverance; protection; intercession; advocacy; confirmation of covenant; comfort; judgment; calling to faith and commitment; provision and safekeeping; representative of God's presence; association with glory cloud; heavenly leader of God's army

Observations:
- May be tied to Pillar of Fire; may be involved in ministry with the Lord Jesus
- Something about coming together with thrones (angels as well); thrones are a power source for them; as travels leaves thrones; thrones in assigned places; they are power source
- May appear as male or female
- May be as many as three Angels of the Lord

Discernment:
- Paul: Like a roaring fire on head where angels are felt
- Jana: Feels as if large and exterior, with pressure on head and atmosphere of fire moving up; sees a lot of light
- Rob: Top of forehead on right side
- Larry: Heat on left side of the neck
- Tobias: Feels an upward whoosh/movement; may see

ANCIENT PATH (4)

Category: Place

History: First prophetic words, November 11, 2003; first discerned, August 28, 2015

Definition: Hebrew: *olam sebil olam:* 439 occurrences; AV translates as 'ever' 272 times, 'everlasting' 63 times, 'old' 22 times, 'perpetual; *sebil*, 'path'[3]

Key Scriptures: Jeremiah 6:16, 18:15

Observations:
- Has been seen going all the way back to Eden and the Tree of Life
- Thrones seem to cooperate with Ancient Path
- All writings of history, and maybe eternity, come together here
- Rivers of information flow through the path
- The gate of entry into life at the beginning when we are created at the womb of dawn, and components of the seed before conception may be discerned here
- Pulsating colors of rainbow; may be able to pick colors to walk on
- We choose way to walk, the freewill part of predestination
- The glorious ones are at foundation of the gate
- Love and joy of Lord of Father regarding His children is here
- May be the place where father and mother issues are resolved
- May be able to take nations there too
- Libraries may be located at the end of Ancient Paths

Discernment:

- Paul: Back, lower half of head

- Jana: Feels presence of Holy Spirit; like crossroads on a portion of the grid that she can walk on

- Larry: Feels a path below him

- Tobias: Lower half of back of head that feels like a trail with a hot river of fire going through it; manifests like a garment heavy on the arm; sees shining angelic writing reminiscent of runes for protection; sometimes reads angelic tongue and becomes interpreter between heaven and earth

APOSTLE (OFFICE) (5)

Category: Being

History: First discerned, early 2000s

Definition: Greek: *apostolos* , 'one sent forth' [4]

Key Scriptures: Ephesians 4:11

Observations:

- Discernment can be either apostolic office or function
- Apostolic strategies given
- Affects the brain/heart/body
- Connects to the eyes of the Lord
- Tied to authority over creation
- Aligns with the ancient path and the library; can go through pathway to library
- May be place where God builds apostolic network
- Connection into land determines where you have apostolic authority

Discernment:

- Paul: Pressure on right or left thumb

- Jana: Right or left thumb with pressure in nail bed

- Rob: Right or left thumb

- Larry: Right or left thumb

- Tobias: Like a battery pack where shoulders and spine come together: feels power in head; felt ancient path/library and apostolic

ARCHANGEL (5A)—SEE ALSO: ANGEL, MICHAEL, GABRIEL

Category: Being

History: First discerned (Michael), 1996; Paul began sensing new archangels being released early 2017

Definition: Greek: *archanggelos*, 'chief angel', a ruler of angels[5]

Key Scriptures: 1 Thessalonians 4:16; Jude 1:9, Daniel 8, 12:1

Observations:

- Different archangels may be discerned individually (i.e. Gabriel, Michael)
- Very strong, like a rock
- May be established or connected to the rock

Discernment:

- Paul: To the left of where angels are felt

- Jana: Feels arch over head with pressure on back shoulder blades, as if armor or wings; in conjunction with a deep, far-off sound

- Larry: Feels great, powerful presence of a being

- Tobias: Feels an upward whoosh; reminded of eagle on a shield; feels like rock being established; feels on right front of head

ARMOR OF LIGHT (6)

Category: God

History: On the evening of August 11, 2010, Paul wrote, "Last night at the movie *Salt* in Collingwood, Canada, the power of God fell and the movie stopped. I got the words, 'His radiant glory' (Hebrews 1:3). The power of God remained on us. Today for the first time I did not feel deliverances while the interns were ministering. I felt His radiant glory the entire time."

Definition: Greek: *hopion*, originally any tool or implement for preparing a thing, became used in the plural for 'weapons of warfare'. Once in the NT it is used of actual weapons, John 18:3; elsewhere, metaphorically, of (a) the members of the body as instruments of unrighteousness and as instruments of righteousness, Rom. 6:13; (b) the 'armor' of light, Rom. 13:12; the 'armor' of righteousness, 2 Cor. 6:7; the weapons of the Christian's warfare, 2 Cor. 10:4[6] *ho phos*, 'of light'. *Apaugasma*, 'radiant', 'a shining forth' (*apo*, 'from', *auge*, 'brightness'), of a light coming from a luminous body, is said of Christ in Heb. 1:3, KJV, 'brightness', RV, 'effulgence', i.e., shining forth (a more probable meaning than reflected brightness).[7]

Key Scriptures: Habakkuk 3:4, Romans 13:12 (armor of light), Hebrews 1:3 (radiant glory)

Characteristics: The Lord covers us with His radiant glory

Functions: Protection and a higher level of deliverance power; appear to be connected to thrones

Observations:

- Primarily light is a luminous emanation, probably of force, from certain bodies, which enables the eye to discern form and color. Light requires an organ adapted for its reception (Matthew 6:22). Where the eye is absent, or where it has become impaired from any cause, light is useless. Man, naturally, is incapable of receiving spiritual light inasmuch as he lacks the capacity for spiritual things (1 Corinthians 2:14). Hence believers are called 'sons of light' (Luke 16:8), not merely because they have received a revelation from God, but because in the New Birth they have received the spiritual capacity for it.[8]

- When armor is correctly adjusted we are rightly connected to Jesus, and indicates how receptive we are

Discernment:

- Paul: Like a rolling fire across the back of head

- Jana: Sees light; feels pressure on shoulder and shoulder blades like wings; feels like energy

- Larry: Feels great power, and inquires what it is
- Tobias: Like a rolling fire across the back of head; also sees like a covering of light; feels a cable being plugged in; feels power packs of two thrones, stronger on right

AUTHORITIES (NOT TO BE CONFUSED WITH AUTHORITY) (7)

Category: Beings

History: First discerned, 2013

Definition: Greek: *exousia,* meaning power, authority, weight, especially: moral authority, influence;[9] freedom of choice, right to act, or decide; the ability to do something, capability, might, power to indicate the thing that is to be done;[10] the lawful right of action and unrestrictive possibility or freedom of action;[11] exert energy, force, might; the power of sway or controlling influence over others.[12]

Key Scriptures: Ephesians 3:10, 6:12; Colossians 2:15; 1 Peter 3:22

Characteristics: Gain knowledge of God's manifold wisdom through the witness of the church; may be righteous or unrighteous

Functions: Involved in spiritual warfare

Observations:
- We believe righteous authorities carry blessings and unrighteous authorities carry curses
- Seers have said that the authorities look like a cube within a cube within a cube within a cube
- May become defiled due to generational anti-Semitism
- They are fractals that go down the generational line
- Need to be submitted to the right authority to discern authorities
- Associated with mantles
- Plug into thrones

Discernment:
- Paul: Back of the head
- Jana: Tingling on either side of head, like effervescence; also

24

has seen carrying a book, scroll, or tablet

- Rob: Pressure on right back side of head (same as Father as Power)
- Larry: Vibration in belly and inquire what it is
- Tobias: Feels to the right side of forehead; also right hip down to knee

AUTHORITY (NOT TO BE CONFUSED WITH AUTHORITIES) (8)

Category: Being

History: First discerned, 1993; one of first things discerned after evil and angels; had put right hand on right thigh and asked the Lord for deliverance

Definition: Greek: *exousia*, 'authority'; from the meaning of 'leave or permission', or liberty of doing as one pleases, it passed to that of 'the ability or strength with which one is endued', to that of the 'power of authority', the right to exercise power[13]

Key Scriptures: Luke 10:19

Characteristics: The authority that one carries that is given by God

Observations: Associated with thrones

Discernment:
- Paul: Intense pressure/anointing on right thigh
- Jana: Sees books and shelves
- Larry: Feeling on left thigh
- Tobias: Like a triangle on top of shoulders

BOOK—SEE ALSO: LIBRARY (9)

Category: Entity

History: Discerned with hand 2005; Head discernment began September 26, 2015

Definition: Hebrew: *seper*, meaning book, letter or scroll; Greek: *biblion*, book or scroll or any sheet on which something is written[14]

Key Scriptures: Exodus 32:33; Numbers 21:14; Psalm 40:7, 69:28,

139:16; Isaiah 29:11-12, 34:16; Ezekiel 3:1-3; Daniel 7:10, 12:1-4; Zachariah 5:1-2; Malachi 3:16; Philippians 4:3; Hebrews 10:7; Revelation 3:5, 5:1-9, 10:2-10, 13:8, 17:8, 20:12-15, 21:27

Characteristics:

- Exist in heavenly places
- Contain all manners of information, both historical and prophetic
- Unlike earthly books (i.e. flying scrolls)
- Some are ancient, written before the foundation of the world
- Seems to be a connection between our spirit and what is in a book; our spirit may be writing the books
- In the library there are scrolls and books, following the historical pattern of development

Functions: Used as reference and/or evidence, used for judgment in heavenly courts, delivered by angels for God's purpose (i.e. to be read or eaten)

Discernment: May be felt as a weight in a hand; shape/size may be felt with the hands; may be seen as a vision

- Paul: Across back ½ of head, like the library; also feels with his hand
- Jana: Sees book
- Larry: Senses scrolls/books
- Tobias: Like a shelf on the ancient path, reminiscent of a ladder but made of multiple shelves instead of rungs; hears phrase, "ladder of revelation"

BRANCH—SEE ALSO: WINDOWS, GRID (10)
Category: Entity

History: Prophetic revelation of the branches of healing began in September and October 2012, including almond branch, pomegranate branch, pear branch, apple branch, olive branch, lime branch, plum branch, peach branch, kumquat branch, orange branch (planted in the conference room) cherry branch, lemon branch; first prophetic dream was in January 2015; first discerned in the spring of 2015.

Definition: Hebrew: *ṣemaḥ,* meaning sprout, growth or branch; thirty-two occurrences of this verb and half as many different translations involving the ideas of growing, budding, and sprouting;[15] Greek: *klema,* meaning shoot or young twig, which is broken off to be replanted, 'slip', 'branch', specifically 'shoot of the vine' [16]

Key Scriptures: Isaiah 11:1, Jeremiah 23:5, Zechariah 3:8, 4:12, John 15:5

Characteristics:

- Spiritual branches have the appearance of a physical branch of a tree
- Branches would be a part of the trees of healing in Ezekiel 47:12 and Revelation 22:2

Functions: Seem to connect a person through windows to the dimensional grid

Observations: Seem connected to thrones; may draw life from them

Discernment:

- Paul: Same as gates, but ½ way from the middle on sides to top back of head (same as thrones and windows); also like pulling sensation on bottom of feet and/or tree coming out of fingers
- Jana: Sees branches; feels pressure on bottom of foot
- Rob: Pressure on bottom of foot
- Larry: Pressure on foot
- Tobias: Sees and then discerns with hands; feels growing out of head; may feel a pulse on bottom of feet

BREAKTHROUGH ANGEL AND/OR BREAKER ANOINTING (11)— SEE ALSO: ANGEL

Category: Being

History: First discerned, 2008

Key Scriptures: 2 Samuel 5:19-21

Observations: May carry the breaker anointing

Discernment:

- Paul: Same as gates but halfway from middle on sides to top back of head (same as thrones and windows); also a pulling sensation on bottom of feet.

- Jana: Pressure on forehead between eyes; pressure on back

- Rob: Like two equidistant bolts on back part of neck

- Larry: Senses being consumed by a being

- Tobias: Feels on shoulders like a pushing of air coming over in waves

BRONZE MAN (12)

Category: Being

Definition: Hebrew: *îš*, 'man', 'mankind', 'champion', 'great man', 'husband', 'person', 'whatsoever', 'whosoever'; [17] *něḥōšet*, 'copper', 'bronze', 'brass', 'brazen'[18]

History: First discerned on July 19, 2014, exactly nine months after a dream on October 19, 2013 that Donna was pregnant; a measuring rod in Paul's left hand and flax in his right hand seen by Larry Pearson; realized it was the bronze man from Ezekiel 40

Key Scriptures: Ezekiel 40, 43

Characteristics:

- A created being, not the Lord

- God's temple is within us and it appears that the enemy places his temple alongside of it; Bronze man measures our dimensions and our temple to make sure we are in right alignment with the God's design, and to show us the correct dimensions and measures

- The Bronze Man measures the bride to determine what is holy and unholy

- Seems tied to four thrones

- After the measuring is finished there is a deliverance of whatever is not right

Functions:

- Larry Pearson, prophetic word: "This measuring rod will be as a plumb line to bring demarcation between what was old to what is coming, what is new, what is not yet seen. A new vision is coming to those who will position themselves at His feet. My measure is looking for my Son. Go and measure those that breathe life and watch the increase. Signs on the earth, signs in the heavens. Signs on the earth release signs in the heaven. There is a new fire abound to release the feet of those that bring good news to release an outpouring."
- The purpose of the measuring is to bring us into the Holy of Holies.
- The measuring also brings us into alignment with justice and righteousness
- The measuring separates the wheat from the tares

Discernment:

- Paul: Two points on left, top side of head (same as Gabriel)
- Jana: Sees a golden figure as a spirit
- Rob: Sensation near top, left side of head
- Larry: Senses a bronze figure in my spirit
- Tobias: Like a "tin man from Oz" standing behind; partial seeing; feels authority and thrones at same time

BURNING BUSH (25)—SEE ETERNITY, I AM

CANDLESTICK (74)—SEE ALSO: POWER

CAPTAIN/COMMANDER OF THE HOST (13)—SEE ALSO: HOST
Category: Being

History: Words about the Captain of the Host started in 2010; first discerned, 2012

Definition: Hebrew: *śar*, 'prince', 'to rule', and *śûr*, 'to hold dominion over'[19] and *ṣĕbā'ôt*, 'armies', 'hosts', thus Captain of the Host (army);[20] same word that is used for prince (i.e. Prince of Persia or Greece in Daniel)

Key Scriptures: Joshua 5:14-15

Characteristics:
We believe the Captain of the Host is a created being and not the Lord; no indication that Joshua worshiped him, but simply says that he worshiped

Observations:
- First appears in the conquest of Israel
- Appearance of the Captain of the Host and the host indicates that warfare has intensified
- Intensifying of the Host and the Captain of Host was discerned after 2012
- Many have seen and also believe he is a created being

Discernment:
- Paul: Right side of head at a point in the middle

- Jana: Pressure on back of head; may hear stars singing

- Rob: Pressure on top of head in two distinct points

- Larry: Knowing in my spirit

- Tobias: Sees him wearing emblems of rank and discerns his authority (clearer and more well defined than host); also sees host (looks humanoid and made of light) behind him; feels him in front on the left

CERTAIN HOLY ONE (69)—SEE ALSO: PALMONI

CHARIOT(S) OF FIRE (14)
Category: Being

History: First discerned, July 15, 2016

Definition: Hebrew: *kebeb*, 'chariot'; *'esh*, translates as 'fire' 373 times, 'burning' once, 'fiery' once, 'flaming' once, and 'hot' once[21]

Key Scriptures: 2 Kings 2:11, 6:17

Observations:

- Intercession of Melchizedek may stir the fire
- A ministry seems to travel in a chariot
- Seems to rescue DID parts
- Seems to be an association with I AM

Discernment:

- Paul: Like two effervescent spots on either side of top middle part of head; also sensation of horses

- Jana: Sees wheels; feels fire moving around

- Larry: Vibration in belly and inquires what is present

- Tobias: Sees big, dense fire in the form a chariot; feels on right elbow, as if in midst of burning bush

CHERUB(IM) (15)

Category: Being

History: First discerned 1992

Definition: Hebrew: *kerub* (ker-oob'), 'cherubim'[22]
Key Scriptures: Genesis 3:24; Exodus 25:17-20, 26:1; 2 Samuel 22:10-11; 1 Kings 6:23-29, 34-35; 1 Chronicles 28:18; 2 Chronicles 3:10-13; Psalm 18:10, 99:1; Isaiah 37:16; Ezekiel 1:4-28, 10:1-22, 28:14-16; 41:17-19; 2 Corinthians 11:14, Revelation 4

Characteristics:

- Living creatures that dwell in the center of the fire in the Cloud of His Presence; Glory of God surrounds them

- Strong wind associated with them

- Look like a man

- Four faces: man, lion, ox, and eagle

- Have four wings (Ezekiel), six wings (Revelation)

- Under wings are two hands of a man

- Each travels straight ahead and does not turn as they move

- Travel as the Spirit travels

- Look like burning coals of fire or torches
- Fire moves back and forth among the creatures
- Burning coals and fire between the wheels
- Lighting flashes out of the fire
- Wheels beside each cherub look like chrysolite. (Strong: a gem, perhaps the topaz; KJV: beryl; NAS: Tarshish stone)
- Wheels appear to intersect each other and do not turn as cherubs move
- Wheels called whirling wheels
- Rims are high and awesome and full of eyes
- An ice expanse over their heads
- Movement of wings sounds like rushing water, voice of the Almighty, the tumult of an army
- Entire body - wings, back, hands, wheels - covered with eyes
- Continually say, "Holy, holy, holy, is the Lord God Almighty who was, and is and is to come."
- Used on Ark of the Covenant and other places throughout the tabernacle/temple

Functions:
- Guardians who carry God's throne; He flies on them
- We may all have personal cherubim and may be moved/transported on them

Observations:
- We do not believe that Lucifer is the cherub mentioned in Ezekiel 28
- Seems to be a connection with thrones

Discernment:
- Paul: Same as angels, but can feel the four heads turning
- Jana: Sees wheels and eyes; pressure on top of head
- Rob: Like a turning wheel on top of head
- Larry: Knowing in my spirit and have to inquire

- Tobias: Feels fire, spinning; may see as indistinct forms

CHROMOSOME (16)

Category: Entity

History: First discerned April 22, 2016

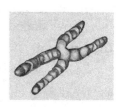

Definition: 23 chromosomes make up the Karyotype or DNA

Key Scriptures: Daniel 2:43

Characteristics: Discernment of damage to chromosomes indicates that they contain evil; when that evil is addressed, deliverance coming off of the chromosomes and genes can be discerned

Observations:
- After prayer to cleanse and restore to God's original intent, testimonies have been received indicating improvement
- Appears to be a spiritual as well as physical strand of DNA
- Connections with stars and thrones

Discernment:
- Paul: Two pressure points on top center of both sides of head; ask the Lord if the issue is from the mother's or father's side

- Jana: Feels energy between 1st finger and thumb; have seen a moving light going in circle

- Tobias: Sees; feels across the chest in front and upper back

CLOUD (17)

Category: Entity

History: First discerned October 26, 2013

Definition: Hebrew: 'ănān, 'cloud'

Key Scriptures: Daniel 7:13, Micah 2:6-13, Matthew 24:30, Mark 13:26, Jude 12, Revelation 1:7

Characteristics: Spiritual clouds seem to be made up of 'word droplets'; evil clouds would be 'clouds without rain'

Observations:
- According to Micah 2:6-13, false words are 'prattler', means droplets; therefore, false words result in ungodly clouds

- Those who come against this evil will go through the Breakthrough Gate.
- We have noticed deliverance occurs when we ask God to remove ungodly clouds from people

Discernment:
- Paul: Like anointing all over head; get a hit saying, 'cloud'
- Jana: Sees sparkles as living waters; feels anointing on top of head
- Rob: Feels ungodly cloud as a sensation between bicep and forearm
- Larry: Senses a cloud and inquires what is present

CLOUD OF WITNESSES (18)

Category: Place

History: First words 2006; unclear when first discerned

Definition: Greek: *nephos,* denotes 'a cloudy, shapeless mass covering the heavens'; hence, metaphorically, of 'a dense multitude, a throng';[23] *martus* or *martur,* (whence Eng., 'martyr', one who bears 'witness' by his death) denotes 'one who can or does aver what he has seen or heard or knows'[24]

Key Scriptures: Hebrews 12:1

Observations: Parts may be in the different dimensions and domains

Discernment:
- Paul: Like a bowl (stadium) on the head; also same as the sons of God
- Jana: Sees sparkles of living water
- Rob: Very strong sensation on top, left side of head
- Larry: Senses people in a cloud
- Tobias: Sees people in the cloud from chest upward, sometimes distinguishes individuals; discerns himself traveling in/through cloud

COUNCIL OF THE LORD (19)

Category: Place

History: First discerned 2012

Definition: Hebrew: *sod*, secret or confidential plan(s); secret or confidential talk; secret; council; gathering; circle. [25]

Key Scriptures: 2 Chronicles 18:19-22, Psalm 89, Jeremiah 23:18

Observations: Thrones seem to surround the council and stars are also present

Discernment:

- Paul: Anointing all over the top of the head, and a hit with 'council'
- Jana: Aware of a circle; sees a color or colors that relate a certain council of the Lord; also sees 7 spirits of God
- Rob: Sensation that covers the head like an overlay from front to back
- Larry: Sense in my spirit and inquire what is present
- Tobias: Sees as semi-circular seating, as in an amphitheater

DEEP (20)

Category: Entity, Place

History: First word received from Persis Tiner on April 14, 2014

Definition: Greek: *bathos* 'deepness'; 'depth' [26]

Key Scriptures: Ephesians 3:18

Characteristics: There seems to be a distinction between the deep and the depth. The deep seems to exist below the depth and seems to be made up of fresh water, as opposed to salt water in the depth. Scientists have actually found a large amount of fresh water under the sea.

Observations: Seems to be the place of water spirits

Discernment:

- Paul: Word of knowledge rather than physical sensation
- Jana: Feels humidity; sometimes hears a sound

- Larry: Sense of being underwater (same as depth) and inquires what is present
- Tobias: Sees as if underneath the ground level of the ocean, with or without water

DEPTH (21)

Category: Entity, Place

History: First discerned, 2008; many people had sense of deep diving suit, high humidity, and going down into water

Definition: Greek: *bathos* 'deepness'; 'depth' [27] (same as Deep)

Key Scriptures: Ephesians 3:18

Characteristics: Place of the soul

Observations: Has been seen as a massive being

Discernment:
- Paul: Top, back half of the head; usually receives a word of knowledge about the depth
- Jana: Word of knowledge; may experience yawning, especially in relation to another person
- Larry: Sense of being underwater (same as the depth) and inquire what is present
- Tobias: Strong sensation on back, like many fingers crawling up; sees as foggy or dusty atmosphere; senses on both sides in front of head; sees red color, as if on a graph, but with much more substance than a line

DOMINION, OR WALL (34)

Category: Being, Place (grid is an extension of the dominion)

History: In the early 1990s, Paul came across an evil force called a dominion that told him it was over material items; increased understanding began November 21, 1996

Definition: Greek: *kuriotes* (koo-ree-ot'-ace), mastery (i.e. concretely and collectively); power or position as lord;[28] supreme authority, sovereignty, absolute ownership;[29] the right and power to govern or judge: authority, command, control, domination, dominion, mastery, might, power, sway, force, weight, rule, supremacy; antonyms: servility, servitude, and weakness; a particular area of activity, study, or interest: specialty, field, area, arena, bag (*slang*), bailiwick, department, domain, dominion, orbit, precinct, province, realm, region, sphere, terrain, territory, and world; legal right to the possession of a thing: title, custody, dominion, entitlement, guardianship, ownership, possession, proprietorship, tenure; an area of land over which rule is exercised: domain, country, dominion, empire, kingdom, land, province, realm, and territory.[30]

Key Scriptures: Ephesians 1:21; Jude 8; other specifically related scriptures below

Characteristics: Has been observed as a covering over the whole earth; ley lines

Functions:

- Being in charge of the grid
- Grid may be an extension of the dominion
- Seem to be aligned with thrones

Observations:

- Appears that a declaration of ownership forms an evil spiritual connection between that object and the person; may vary from small item to large land mass; seems that personal declaration of ownership in essence gives over a piece of property to the enemy (i.e. high place, forming an ungodly spiritual connection other ungodly connections (i.e. ley lines) can be affected; the evil that is involved may be a fallen dominion
- The spiritual connections between a person and their possessions may explain how psychics can find an individual by holding unto one of their possessions; perhaps they can see the spiritual connections
- Scripture is clear that all belongs to the Lord (Job 41:11; Psalm 22:27-28, 24:1; 1 Corinthians 10:26) and we are to rule over creation in His name (Genesis 1:26-28)
- When we sinned we gave over to the enemy what was God's (Leviticus 25:23)

- Highways of Holiness appear to be managed by righteous dominions and ley lines are managed by unrighteous dominions

Discernment:

- Paul: Feels something like an H on top of head as a living grid

- Jana: Sees grid; explores by feeling lines that connect

- Rob: Feels dimensional shifting on the fight side of the nose and inquires where

- Larry: Senses path below feet and inquire what is present

- Tobias: Looks like a huge spacecraft and hears sound like metal stress; feels power going through legs

DOOR (22)

Category: Entity

History: First revelation 2011; first discerned early 2016

Definition: Hebrew: *delet*, door, leaf (of a door); this noun used eighty-six times in the OT and in all but one passage it refers to the door on a house, a room of the house, a temple, or the gates of a city; sometimes it is used metaphorically;[31] Greek: *thura*, 'a door'[32]

Key Scriptures: Isaiah 45:1-2, Revelation 3:20, 4:1

Characteristics:

- Doors can be closed by the enemy when they should be opened

- Doors can be opened by the enemy when they should be closed

- Righteous doors are to be opened so the gates will remain open

- Stars and doors appear to be connected through thrones

Functions: Openings into kingdoms within the dimensions

Observations: When comparing doors and gates it is essential to look at the original Hebrew word in the text; often the words are mistranslated.

Discernment:

- Paul: Like parallel bars on back, left and right edges of head; feels stars at the same time
- Jana: Sees a blue flash and/or door
- Rob: Left, big toe
- Larry: Knowing in my spirit and inquires what is present
- Tobias: Feels strong door over his heart and on right side of head toward the back; sees doors

DOORKEEPER (35)—SEE GATEKEEPER

ELDER (23)

Category: Being

History: First discerned early 2003

Definition: Greek: *presbuteros* (pres-boo' ter-os); comparative of *presbus* (elderly); 'older'; as noun, 'a senior'; specifically, an Israelite Sanhedrist (also figuratively, member of the celestial council) or Christian 'presbyter': KJV 'elder' (-est), old[33]

Key Scriptures: Revelation 4:10, 5:5-14, 7:11, 7:13, 11:16, 14:3, 19:4

Characteristics:

- 24 located around the throne of God
- Also, 24 appear at different levels around marriages, families, churches, cities, states, etc.
- Some see appearance of evil elders similar to leprechauns or gnomes
- Personal elders out of alignment may have to do with gender confusion
- Seem to be both male and female elders around the throne

Functions:

- Worship
- Often the ones who touch a person in a place on their body where they are to pray for healing for others
- Seem to influence DNA and RNA

Discernment:

- Paul: Back, left side of head
- Jana: Feels touch on left side of head or face
- Rob: Back, left side of head right above the neck
- Larry: Knowing in my spirit and inquire what is present
- Tobias: Sees what look like small people with beards, both male and female

ELEMENTAL SPIRIT (24)

Category: Being

History: Felt profound cold the first time discerned, early 2000s

Definition:

- Hebrew: *Stoicheia* (stoy-khi'-on): something orderly in arrangement, i.e. (by implication) a serial (basal, fundamental, initial) constituent (literally), proposition (figuratively): Basic elements such as letters of alphabet or basic elements of universe – earth, air, fire, water.[34]
- Clinton Arnold - the interpretation of *stoicheia* as personal spiritual entities is the most common view; was used for astral spirits in 2nd and 3rd century, "I conjure you by the 12 *stocheia* of heaven and the 24 *stoicheia* of the world in order that you would lead me to Hercules."
- *stoicheion*, used in the plural, primarily signifies any first things from which others in a series, or a composite whole take their rise; the word denotes "an element, first principle" (from *stoichos*, "a row, rank, series"); *stoicheia* reflects a common Hellenistic and Jewish view that certain cosmic entities or astral powers were set over the four elements, the planets, and the stars.[35]

Key Scriptures: Galatians 4:3-5, 9; Colossians 2:8, 20

Characteristics: Spiritual beings behind the elements on the periodic table

Functions:

- Seem to be neutral spiritually

- It appears they can be contaminated and then affect the normal functioning of the physical elements on the periodic table.
- Appear to connect to the Glory of God by the glorious ones (*doxa*)

Observations: Have to do with basic principles of the world

Discernment:

- Paul: Top, back of neck
- Jana: Feels cold, like a surrounding cloud; back of neck tingles
- Rob: Like a line across the back, top of head
- Larry: Senses pressure under feet
- Tobias: Feels at back of head like little cubes moving around; usually sees as small cubes, often with name of element and/or math equations written on them

ENCOURAGEMENT (28)—SEE EXHORTATION

ETERNITY (25): SEE ALSO, I AM, BURNING BUSH

Category: God

History: First discerned on July 15, 2016, as the burning bush and knew it was the center of I AM. It became clear on September 30, 2016, that it was I AM as well as eternity when the burning bush showed up at the end of an Academy and was identified as the center of I AM. It was like rotating fire flowing ever inward. El Shaddai was in the center. The bush also seems to be in the center of Mt. Zion and seems to be where the transfiguration was.

Definition: Hebrew: *olam*, 'everlasting', 'eternity'; [36] Greek: *aion*, signifies a period of indefinite duration[37]

Key Scriptures: Ecclesiastics 3:11; 2 Peter 3:18

Characteristics:

- Seems to be the location of Mt. Zion
- Exists outside of time
- Connection between heaven and earth
- Located in the heart of God and in the human heart (physical,

soul, and spirit)

- Jesus is the door into I AM

Discernment:

- Paul: Bar-like pressure on middle of head from right to left

- Jana: Word of knowledge; sees picture of a horizon; if burning bush, sees horizon, and stepping into it feels like being in the midst of fire; tests this with Hebrew name of God in the midst, 'Elohim Gereb'

- Rob: Feels horizontal bar across top of head

- Larry: Feels encased in a powerful being and have to inquire what is present

- Tobias: Sees golden glory stream, like lines of light streaming out of the Lord; if unrighteous, sees a closed loop, like infinity symbol

EVANGELIST (OFFICE) (26)

Category: Being

History: First discerned, early 2000s

Definition: Greek: *euangelistes,* 'a messenger of good, a preacher of the gospel' [38]

Key Scriptures: Ephesians 4:11

Observations: Discernment can represent office or function, and may also represent evangelism.

Discernment:

- Paul: Pressure on right or left middle finger

- Jana: Pressure on the middle finger; feels anointing coming up from the feet of a person like a flowing river

- Rob: Pressure on the middle finger

- Larry: Pressure on the middle finger on either side

- Tobias: Left middle finger; sees and feels a man standing on top of the head with a funnel around him that has something coming out of it and a staff in his hand

EVIL (DEFAULT)
Discernment (See appendix 2):

- Paul: A point on the back, left side of the head

- Jana: Left side behind the ear

- Larry: Left front forehead is prickly

- Tobias: Top, right back of head

EXHORTATION OR ENCOURAGEMENT (SPIRITUAL GIFT) (28)
Category: Being

History: First discerned early 1990s

Definition: Greek: *paraklesis*, 'a calling to one's side'; hence, either an exhortation, consolation or comfort [39]

Key Scriptures: Romans 12:8; Hebrews 3:13

Discernment:

- Paul: Like a river that seems to have rapids flowing through the mouth of a person, and discerned from far behind to far ahead

- Jana: Anointing from the mouth like a flowing river

- Rob: Sensation over mouth

- Larry: Quivering on my mouth and have to inquire what is present, same as eagle/spirit of prophecy

- Tobias: Feels coming out of mouth

FATHER AS POWER (29)
Category: God

History: First discerned May 17, 2013

Definition: Greek: *dunamis*, 'power, ability', physical or moral, as residing in a person or thing; 'power in action', as, e.g., when put forth in performing miracles; occurs 118 times in the NT; is sometimes used of the miracle or sign itself, the effect being put for the cause. [40]

Key Scriptures: Matthew 26:64; Acts 1:8

Characteristics: The Father in His everlasting omnipotent power

Discernment:

- Paul: Strongly on back of head

- Jana: Feels very powerful on back of neck

- Rob: Right, back side of head

- Larry: Powerful Being and have to inquire what is present

- Tobias: Sees like a sphere with light inside of it, like a fusion reaction; feels moving in a circle around his head

FEMALENESS (30)

Category: God, Being, Entity, Place

History: First discerned, 2015

Definition: Hebrew: *nĕqēbâ,* 'female'; Greek: *thḗlus,* 'female'[41]

Key Scriptures: Genesis 1:27, Matthew 19:4

Discernment:

- Paul: When placing hand on the left side of the body, get a hit saying, "female"

- Tobias: Feels on right side of brain

FIERY STONES (31)

Category: Entity

History: First prophetic words, 2010; first discerned, Sept 21, 2015

Definition: Hebrew: *'esh eben,* 'fiery' [AV translates as 'fire' 373 times, 'burning' once, 'fiery' once, 'untranslated variant' once, 'fire + 800' once, 'flaming' once, and 'hot' once; 1 fire; 1A fire, flames; 1B supernatural fire (accompanying theophany); 1C fire (for cooking, roasting, parching); 1D altar-fire; 1E God's anger[42]

Key Scriptures: Ezekiel 28:14,16; Galatians 4:3,9; Colossians 2:8,20

Characteristics: Seem to consist of all components of physical matter, atomic and sub atomic particles

Observations: The manifestation of fiery stones is what began Larry Pearson's healing of Crohn's Disease in August 2010.

Discernment:

- Paul: Vibrations on the back of my head

- Jana: Sees them; feels vibration on bottom of feet

- Rob: Burning sensation on right, back of head above neck

- Larry: Strong sense of them under feet and can be standing on them often in the realm; has at times been sensed being dipped in and out of them with a sense of hot and cool

- Tobias: Like updraft of heated air; sees like glowing hot stones, such as used for massage

FURNACE (32)—SEE ALSO: ANGEL OF THE LORD

Category: Being

History: First discerned, 2001

Definition: Hebrew: *tannûr* furnace, oven;[43] *ṣārap* smelt, refine, test[44] and *'esh* (aysh) fire,[45] refiner's fire

Key Scriptures: Malachi 3:2, 4:1

Characteristics: A burning fire that results in intense deliverance and purification

Observations:

- A man walked through the furnace during our first tent meeting at the Victorian House in Hesperia and was healed of brain cancer

- A woman who was DID walked through the furnace and was integrated

Discernment:

- Paul: Left top head, (same as Angel of the Lord)

- Jana: May see as a square fire; feels heat in front of her

- Rob: Intense fire-like sensation over face

- Larry: Burning in belly and inquire what is present

- Tobias: See as oven; feels heat

GABRIEL (33)—SEE ALSO: ANGEL, ARCHANGEL

Category: Being

History: First word April, 2004; Discerned Hayward, CA in 2010

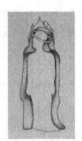

Definition: Hebrew *Gabriel* [46] means 'God is my strength' [47]

Key Scriptures: Daniel 8:16-17, 9:21-22; Luke 1:19, 26–27, 34-35

Characteristics: Archangel; stands in the presence of God

Functions:

- Messenger—delivered messages to Daniel, Zacharias, and Mary
- We have noticed he often escorts one into the dimensions
- Delivers and interprets messages

Discernment:

- Paul: Two points on left top, left side of the head

- Jana: Feels as if inside, with a heavier weight of pressure on my head than an angel; physically feels as if all energy has left my body; much revelation follows

- Rob: Sensation over right temple

- Larry: Powerful being and have to inquire what is present

- Tobias: Often feels first as very big and strong, along with a sense of goodness of heart; then sees in part due to huge size, and may appear dressed similar to a Viking warrior who may be flying with one arm extended as if breaking through

GATE (22)—SEE ALSO: DOMINION, DOORS, GRID

Category: Entity

History: First revelation 2011; first discerned early 2016

Definition: Hebrew: *sarar*, root idea is 'to split open' (so the verb in Ethiopic), 'to break through' (so the Arabic); two other words are sometimes translated 'gate' *petah* and *delet*; former actually means 'entrance,' from the verb meaning 'to open'; latter refers to

46

the 'door leaves' making up part of the gate; *ša'ar* refers to the whole gate complex and to the open area on either side of it;[48] Greek: *pule* is used (a) literally, for a larger sort of 'gate,' in the wall either of a city or palace or temple, Luke 7:12, of Nain (burying places were outside the 'gates' of cities); Acts 3:10; 9:24; 12:10; Heb. 13:12; (b) metaphorically, of the 'gates' at the entrances of the ways leading to life and to destruction; importance and strength of 'gates' made them viewed as synonymous with power [49]

Key Scriptures: Genesis 22:17, 24:60; Psalm 24; Isaiah 26:2, 45:1-2; Proverbs 8:3; Mathew 16:18

Characteristics: Many have seen all kinds of gates in the spirit; often they have a sign on the lintel designating the purpose of the gate; gatekeepers stand by the gate; often there are blood, threshold, and salt covenants written on the base of the gate; writing often in Hebrew

Functions: Openings on the grid to allow access to doors and kingdoms

Observations:
- You can tell different kinds of gates by asking the Lord what gate it is, and then getting a hit if you are correct
- If the gate is unrighteous, the doors after the gate need to be dealt with first; unrighteous doors need to be closed and righteous doors need to be opened
- A star (being) often functions as a gate or a door

Discernment:
- Paul: Parallel bars on the back of the left and right edges of head
- Jana: Sees two pillars or posts; feels pressure on top of head
- Rob: Left big toe
- Larry: Senses something in front of me and have to inquire what is present
- Tobias: Sees a variety of styles similar to physical appearances; feels pulsating sensation on both sides of head in back

GATEKEEPER, OR DOORKEEPER (35)

Category: Being

History: First discerned, early 2010s

Definition:

Key Scriptures: Isaiah 22:22; Revelation 3:7-9

Functions: Similar tasks but assigned to gates or doors; evil gatekeepers/doorkeepers block entrance to gates/doors we should have entrance to

Observations:

- Those who guarded gates of the cities and doors of palaces, temples, and other large buildings.
- Task was to admit or reject visitors (2 Kings 7:10–11; 11:4–9).
- In the Bible these men are variously named as gatekeepers, porters, doorkeepers, and guards.[50]
- There appear to be spiritual beings who hold the keys to the gates and doors that have this function on the grid

Discernment:

- Paul: A vibration on the lower portion of the back of my neck; feels with hand on either side of gate/door
- Jana: Sees being standing next to two pillars; feels pressure on back of head
- Rob: Back of head
- Larry: Senses a being in front of me and have to inquire what is present

GIVING (SPIRITUAL GIFT) (36)

Category: Being

History: First discerned, early 1990s

Definition: Greek: *metadíd mi* - to give[51]

Key Scriptures: Romans 12:8, Luke 6:38

Discernment:

- Paul: Like a river with rapids flowing through the elbows of a person and discerned from far behind to far ahead

- Jana: Anointing flowing from forearms
- Rob: Forearm

GLORIOUS ONES (37)
Category: Being

History: First discerned, 2007

Definition: Hebrew: *doxa*, primarily denotes 'an opinion, estimation, repute'; in the NT, always 'good opinion, praise, honor, glory, an appearance commanding respect, magnificence, excellence, manifestation of glory'; hence, of angelic powers, in respect of their state as commanding recognition, 'dignities,' 2 Pet. 2:10; Jude 8; see glory, honor, praise, worship[52]

Key Scriptures: Exodus 33:18; 1 Peter 2:10; Jude 8

Characteristics: Seem to be living light beams that are the foundation of life

Observations:
- Appear to connect the elemental spirits (which are connected to the physical elements of our body) to the Glory of God
- Hold the frequency of the original design

Discernment:
- Paul: Bar across top, back of head from side to side
- Jana: Feels like an angelic hand on the middle of head
- Rob: Ping-Pong-like sensation over front of head
- Larry: Powerful beings and have to inquire what is present
- Tobias: Sensation across the middle of back, with sense of a minty essential oil; also across top, back right side of head; sees as similar appearance to atoms and electrons with glory and light in/on it; may sense them reacting behind him under shoulder blades

GLORY OF GOD (38)
Category: God

History: First discerned on May 16, 2015 in Ireland; two friends saw two horns they felt were connected to the grid; first discerned the horns on October 22, 2016 while on the North Shore of Oahu and realized it was the Glory of God

Definition: Hebrew: *kabod,* glory [53] Greek: *doxa,* primarily denotes 'an opinion, estimation, repute'; in the NT, always 'good opinion, praise, honor, glory, an appearance commanding respect, magnificence, excellence, manifestation of glory'[54]

Key Scriptures: Exodus 33:18; John 1:14; Habakkuk 3:4

Observations: Glory on Moses' face came from the glory of the letters of the law written on the stone (2 Corinthians 3:7-8)

Discernment:

- Paul: Two streams flowing up on the top back part of my head, like two bolts on the left and right sides; like horns of Moses

- Jana: Feels weight on sides and top of head; feels a vibrating field abound her

- Rob: Two equidistant points on back of head

- Larry: Feel a weighty presence and a deep stillness

- Tobias: Sees as golden, intense radiation

GOLDEN BOWL (39)
Category: Entity

History: First discerned, 2005

Definition: Hebrew: *zahab,* (zaw-hawb'): gold;[55] Greek: *gullah* (gool-law'): a basin, bowl[56]

Key Scriptures: Ecclesiastes 12:6, Zechariah 4:1-4

Characteristics: Sits atop the golden lampstand, and is a receptacle for the golden oil; prayers of saints seem to be in these bowls (Revelation 5:8) and contamination of prayers can be discerned

Discernment:

- Paul: Like a circular bowl on head; feels with hands on other people

- Jana: Sees a gold bowl with Hebrew writing that is transparent
- Larry: Feels like a bowl on my head
- Tobias: Sees as a golden bowl on top of head

GOLDEN PIPES (40)

Category: Being

History: First discerned October 17, 2014, Kaneohe, Hawaii; a lady had come in for prayer later reported that her hips and her knuckles had been healed; the power of God was very intense.

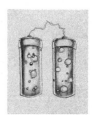

Definition: Hebrew: *zāhāb*, gold*;* *ṣantĕrôt*, pipes

Key Scriptures: Zechariah 4:12, correctly translated as, "Who are these two spikes of the olive trees which are in the hands of the two pressers of gold–the ones who express the gold from (the olives) on them."

Functions: Seem to function as transducers (devices that convert one form of energy (sound, temperature, light etc.) into an electrical signal (voltage, current etc.); we have noticed that when pipes and discerned and functioning, the deliverance intensifies

Observations: Connected to thrones

Discernment:

- Paul: Feels like parallel vertical rods on the back of my head; often an intense burning feeling
- Jana: Sees them
- Rob: Back of head
- Larry: Like Paul, with intense heat
- Tobias: Sees as described; feels like they are boiling

GLORY REALM (41)

Category: God

History: First discerned, September 12, 2015

Definition: Hebrew: *kabod*, 'glory'

Key Scriptures: Exodus 24:16, 33:18, Matthew 25:31

Observations: Not just where God is, but goes to God as I AM; healing is felt here

Discernment:

- Paul: Like a waterfall flowing inward on the top of my head
- Jana: Feels an energy field and a heaviness on back of neck
- Rob: Two equidistant points on back of head
- Larry: A powerful expanse below my feet
- Tobias: Feels multiple beings within the realm

GRID (82)—SEE HIGHWAYS OF HOLINESS, DOMINION

HEALING (42)
Category: Being

History: First discerned in 1993

Definition: Greek: *iama*, 'a healing' (the result of the act), used in the plural, in 1 Cor. 12:9, 28, 30 [57]

Key Scriptures: 1 Corinthians 12:28-30

Characteristics: Also a spiritual gift

Observations: May be make or female

Discernment:

- Paul: Palm of my hand, especially the left
- Jana: Burning on upper palm of left hand
- Rob: Fire in hands
- Larry: Center of the palm of my hand either left or right
- Tobias: Feels heaviness of left shoulder; sometimes feels like a stream or presence; sees as a person with a sort of body armor

HEIGHT (43)
Category: Being, Place (Domain)

History: First discerned, May 26, 2010

Definition: Greek: *húpsos*, 'height', 'elevation'[58]

Key Scriptures: Ephesians 3:18

Characteristics: Place of ruling and reigning

Observations: Has been seen as a massive being

Discernment:

- Paul: ½ towards the back of my head, usually with a word of knowledge, "height" when I am to focus on the height
- Rob: Discerns dimensional shifting and inquires where
- Tobias: Sees yellow color, as if on a graph, but with much more substance than a line

HIGHWAYS OF HOLINESS (44)—SEE ALSO DOMINION AND PATHWAYS

Category: Entity

History: Early 1990's

Definition: Hebrew: *derek,* 'way', 'road'[59]

Key Scriptures: Isaiah 35:8

Observations:

- Spiritual beings seem to travel on these lines (highways)
- At the intersections are gates that go into dimensions

Discernment:

- Paul: Grid lines (like graph paper), which I feel in the air; contaminated lines are ley lines.
- Jana: Word of knowledge; sees paths and lines; feels path as anointing going up
- Larry: Feel in the air
- Tobias: Sees like tubes you can travel along

HOLINESS (45)

Category: Being

History: First discerned, July 9, 2014

Definition: Hebrew: *qodesh,* 'holy'; verb connotes the state of that which belongs to the sphere of the sacred; thus it is distinct from the common or profane[60] Greek *émprosthen*

Key Scriptures: Exodus 15:11; 2Chronicles 31:18; Psalms 60:6,

89:35, 93:5,108:7; Ezekiel 28:25; Romans 1:4; 2 Corinthians 1:12; 2 Corinthians 7:1; Ephesians 4:24; 1Thessalonians 3:13; Hebrews 12:10

Characteristics: Associated with healing, realignment; root of evangelism

Discernment:

- Paul: Vibration on the left side of head below my ear, close to where I feel Jesus as the Son of Man
- Jana: Feels energy on right side, like Jesus as Son of Man standing there
- Larry: Overwhelming presence of purity
- Tobias: Sees with thick, curly, should-length hair the is alive and full of upward movement

HOLY SPIRIT (PERSON OF HOLY SPIRIT) (46)
Category: God

History: First discerned December 21, 2012

Definition: Greek: *hagios pneuma,* 'Holy Spirit'

Key Scriptures: John 14:17, 26; 15:26; 1 Corinthians 2:10,11; 12:11

Discernment:

- Paul: Feels like an effervescence on left, top side of head
- Jana: Feels like holiness with breath and a person on right or left side
- Rob: Feels on left, back top of head
- Larry: Feels a powerful, surrounding Presence
- Tobias: Feels on left upper quadrant of back; may feel standing in front of him; hears as a subtle voice in the head and a sense in emotions, almost as if someone inside is saying the words

HONEY (47)
Category: Entity

History: Frequent words/references since 2005; first discerned April, 2011

Definition: Hebrew: *debash,* (deb-ash'), 'honey'[61]

Key Scriptures: Genesis 43:11; Exodus 3:8; 16:31; Deuteronomy 32:13; Psalm 19:9-11, 119:103; Proverbs 5:3, 16:24, 24:13-14, 25:16, 2:17; Song of Solomon 4:11, 5:3; Ezekiel 3:3; Revelation 10:9-10

Characteristics: Manifestation seems to be tied to deliverance and healing; appearance often signifies revelation

Observations: May refer to food, describe the sweetness of the land of Canaan, or illustrate biblical lessons

Discernment:

- Paul: Feels like hands are sticky and appear shiny

- Jana: None

- Larry: Sticky substance in the hands

- Tobias: Feels it all over us, as if in a room where everything is sticky; sees as real honey

HORNS (38)—SEE GLORY OF GOD

HORSE (48)

Category: Being

History: First discerned September 20, 2011 in Gillette, WY

Definition: Hebrew: *sus,* 'horse'

Key Scriptures: Zechariah 1:7-17; Job 39:18-25

Characteristics: Seems to carry us within the dimensions to other places within that dimension

Discernment:

- Paul: Feels like anointing all over head

- Jana: Sees horses

- Rob: Galloping sensation on head

- Larry: Galloping feeling; sometimes hears them

- Tobias: Sees them, often pawing and eager to run; often feels their power and strength; may see us on horses.

HOST (49)

Category: Being

History: First discerned, 2012

Definition: Hebrew: *ṣābā,* 'fight', 'serve', 'war', 'army'; *ṣĕbā'ôt,* 'armies', 'hosts' (RSV and ASV are similar; ASV uses 'hosts' more often, while RSV uses 'army', 'service', or 'company'; for 'Lord of hosts' ASV uses 'Jehovah of hosts' and NIV uses 'Lord Almighty'; note Rev 4:8) [62]

Key Scriptures: Exodus 12:41; Deuteronomy 4:19; Joshua 5:13-14; Psalm 24:10; Daniel 8:11-12

Characteristics:

- 'Host' may imply either singular or plural
- Appear to made up of warlike spiritual beings that appear humanoid
- Host of heaven seems to include the host, angelic armies, watchers, stars, holy ones, mighty ones, and both the deceased and living saints

Discernment:

- Paul: Top, left middle of head
- Jana: Hears stars singing; word of knowledge
- Rob: Middle, left, top of the head

I AM (25)—SEE ALSO: BURNING BUSH, ETERNITY

JEHOVAH JIREH, OR YAHWEH JIREH (50)

Category: God

History: First discerned September 24, 2014; confirmed with prophetic word September 27, 2014

Definition: Hebrew: *yeh·ho·vaw yir·eh*, 'The Lord Will Provide'

Key Scriptures: Genesis 22:14

Discernment:

- Paul: Left side of head about one inch from left ear

- Tobias: Sees a hand at the ceiling dropping coins like huge CDs; sees and feels warmth of food and cars running

KAIROS (51)

Category: Being

History: First discerned, 2012, when Paul felt with hand something like a 15-20 foot foot-span with sand flowing through an hourglass; received a message from time, and seemed like first time that Time had communicated with a human being

Definition: Greek: *kairos*, primarily, 'a due measure,' is used of 'a fixed and definite period, a time, season,' and is translated 'opportunity.' [63]

Key Scriptures: Galatians 6:10, Ephesians 5:16, Hebrews 11:15

Observations:

- In a spiritual sense, the Lord seems to indicate that Kairos is His time as opposed to man's time, which is Chronos

- Chronos is used in a natural way to signify time; but in discernment, Kairos is righteous and Chronos is god of time

Discernment:

- Paul: An effervescent sensation (same as angels); a hit saying, "Kairos" (feels Chronos same way, along with default evil)

- Rob: A fizzy sensation emanating skyward from top, front of head

- Tobias: Sees as hourglass; may see as a river flowing with many tributaries

LAW (52)

Category: Being

History: First discerned March 3, 2017

Definition: Hebrew: *torah*, 'law', 'direction', 'instruction'[64] Greek: *nomos*, 'usage', 'custom', and then, 'law', as decreed by a state and set up as the standard for the administration of justice.[65]

Key Scriptures: Psalm 119; Romans 8:2; 1 Corinthians 15:56; 2 Corinthians 3:7-11; Hebrews 7:19, 28.

Discernment:

- Paul: Discern I AM plus two lines going to the back of my head like a goal post

- Rob: Across front half of head

LEADER (SPIRITUAL GIFT) (53)
Category: Being

History: First discerned, early 1990s

Definition: Greek: *proistemi*, 'to preside rule', also means 'to maintain' [66]

Key Scriptures: Romans 12:8; 1 Timothy 3:4, 5

Discernment:

- Paul: Like a river with rapids flowing over the shoulders of a person that can be discerned from far behind to far ahead

- Jana: Anointing like a river coming off the head

- Rob: Strong sensation on shoulders

LENGTH (54)
Category: Entity, Place

History: First discerned, 2011

Definition: Greek: *mékos*, 'length'[67]

Key Scriptures: Ephesians 3:18

Characteristics: Place of sexual oneness

Observations: A young man who had been in an illicit sexual relationship with a woman shared, "As soon as I had started this relationship with her I realized that I had stepped outside of that space where God is and evil surrounded me. Wanting to get back to that space, I broke off the relationship."

Discernment:

- Paul: Feels like a bar across the middle of my head, most often with a word of knowledge when I am to focus on the length

- Jana: Word of knowledge

- Rob: Feels dimensional shifting and inquires of Lord

LEY LINES (44)—SEE HIGHWAYS OF HOLINESS

LIBRARY (55)—SEE ALSO: BOOK(S), LENGTH, WIDTH, HEIGHT, DEPTH, LIGHTNINGS, PILLAR

Category: Place

History: Dreams in 2005, 2006, 2010; discerned September 26, 2015; ongoing revelation 2016

Definition: 'Library' not found in Scripture, so the inference is that when there are books they are contained in the library

Key Scriptures: Genesis 5:1; Exodus 17:14, 32:33; Numbers 21:14; Ezra 4:15; Psalms 40:7, 69:28, 139:16; Isaiah 29:11-12, 34:16; Daniel 7:10, 9:2, 12:1-4; Malachi 3:16; Philippians 4:3; Hebrews 10:7; Revelation 3:5, 5:1-9, 10:2-10, 13:8, 17:8, 20:12-15, 21

Characteristics:

- Seen in the spirit as a typical library with bookcases that contain both scrolls and books
- There are pillars in the library
- Appears that the librarians are scribes

Functions: A repository of all words, thought or spoken, by a person

Observations:

- The library functions as a repository of all that is thought and said not only by a person but by those in the generational line
- Words of those in the generational line impact individuals now
- Seems to be a library for each person, but also there are generational libraries so it seems a person is connected to the

libraries of parents, great parents, etc.

- Seems to contain the original design found in the DNA and RNA of each person
- There are maps in the libraries.
- Whole library system is multi-dimensional
- Enemy also seems to have research libraries to find rights to come against a person, which contains information based on the Tree of the Knowledge of Good and Evil
- On many occasions the Lord has instructed us to ask Him to destroy the ungodly library
- May be different libraries in the length, width, height and depth
- Seem to be legal libraries
- The lightnings of God have been discerned in the library
- There is a unique library on Mt. Zion with I AM, and in the creation court
- Seems to be a scribe (librarian) in the library

Discernment:

- Paul: Like two parallel bars on each side of top of head, halfway back; librarian like two parallel bars on each side of the top of head, one half from the front
- Jana: See books and shelves
- Rob: Back half of head
- Larry: Feels pathways under feet and inquires what is present
- Tobias: Sees books, shelves

LIGHTNINGS (56)
Category: Entity

History: First discerned around 1994 while in Apple Valley, CA. At that time I (Paul) did not know what I was feeling, but experienced intervals of pulses as pressure on my head near where I feel angels. The regular pulses at around 90-second intervals lasted for two days, after which the Lord released a strong anointing that caused me to fall to the ground under strong surges of energy. It was not until 2013, that I realized I was feeling lighting strikes.

Definition: Hebrew: *bārāq*, 'lightning', Greek: *astrape*, 'lightning'[68]

Key Scriptures: Psalm 18:14; Revelation 4:5

Observations: Deliverance occurs with lightning strikes

Discernment:

- Paul: Sensation is not sudden, as in earthly lighting, but is a strong pressure that increases and gradual lessens (close to angel's spot)

- Jana: Sees a flash

- Rob: Feels lightning strikes on top, left side of head

- Larry: Sees a flashing presence

- Tobias: Hears a high frequency sound

LION OF JUDAH (27)

Category: God

History: First discerned summer of 2016

Key Scriptures: Revelation 5:5

Characteristics: Connected to healing, majesty, strong but also gentle and kind

Observations: Often seen walking around in a gathering

Discernment:

- Paul: Bottom left and right on the back of head like two pressure points

- Jana: Sees a lion

- Larry: Knowing in my spirit that a Lion is present

- Tobias: Sees and feels Him walking around and rubbing against him; seems very loving, strong, and can be gentle or ferocious

LITTLE SCROLL (OR BOOK) (57)

Category: Entity

History: First discerned February 14, 2016; discerned independently the next day by Rob Gross

Definition: Greek: *bibliarídion*, 'small roll or volume', 'a little scroll'[69]

Key Scriptures: Revelation 10:2, 8–10

Characteristics: This book, which seems to be a cylinder, is carried by the Rainbow Angel and seems to hold mathematical equations and DNA and RNA information

Observations: Seems to be tied to: revival, reformation, revolution; the fivefold ministry, which will bring the Body of Christ into the unity of faith, the knowledge of the Son of God, and maturity or the fullness of Christ; the Mazzaroth; scripture indicates revelation of the little book is an end-time indicator

Discernment:

- Paul: A rolling sensation across back of head

- Jana: Sees a scroll

- Rob: Middle indentation of neck

- Larry: Sees a scroll

- Tobias: Sees a book

LIVING WORD (58)

Category: Being

History: First discerned 5/16/16

Definition: Greek: *zao*, 'to live', 'be alive'[70]

Key Scriptures: Hebrew 4:12

Characteristics:

- Has been seen as a sword, the sharpness of which looks like a diamond; sword also seems to be a living being tied to the Living Word; seems to be between a male and female angel; purpose seems that everything that can be divided in a righteous way

- Seems to be a connection with the Tree of Life

- Energy tied to the Living Word seems to be electromagnetic

- Seems to be tied with the concept of a working force which is the word 'powerful' in Hebrews 4:12 and has to do with faith

Discernment:

- Paul: Feel to the right of holy ones; a sparkling that has to do with 'living'; in the same place as angels

- Jana: Sees rainbow colors around words.

- Larry: Senses a sword in my spirit and inquire what is present

- Tobias: Feels as a dense force in the atmosphere that sends out gravitational waves

MAJESTY (59)—SEE ALSO: SERAPHIM

Category: Place

History: Discerned January 16, 2015

Definition: Hebrew; *ga'ăwâ*, 'majesty'; *hadar*, 'glory', *hod*, 'majesty', 'splendor', 'glory', 'honor'; *gaon*, 'splendor', 'majesty', 'glory'; Greek; *megalosyne*, 'majesty', 'loftiness'; English; 'regal', 'lofty', 'stately dignity', 'imposing character' 'grandeur'[71]

Key Scriptures: Deuteronomy 33:26, 33:29; 1 Chronicles 16:27, 29:11; Job 40:9-10; Psalm 8:4-5, 21:3, 45:1-4, 68:34, 90:16, 93:1-2, 96:6, 104:1, 145:4-12; Isaiah 2:10, 2:19, 2:21, 24:14, 26:10, 35:2; Hebrews 1:2-4, 8:1-2; 2 Peter 1:16; Jude 25

Characteristics:

- Seems to be a realm (domain) where billions of seraphim are worshiping with the saints and many angels.

- Place of God's throne; location of God's greatness and intense glory; place where God fights for the saints; place where His superior strength and power is located

- May be location of the paths of the saints

- Lord's glory is placed on the saints

Discernment:

- Paul: Like two bolts on left and right side at top, back of head

- Jana: A plane through head about eyebrow level, like an oval disk with a lot of lines going out from it that feel almost like a sunrise in head; sees colorful horizon sunrise and aware of translucent colors

- Rob: Two equidistant points on back of head
- Larry: Powerful surrounding presence and inquire what is present

MALENESS (60)

Category: God, Being, Entity, Place

History: First discerned 2015

Definition: Hebrew: *zākār,* 'male', Greek: *arsēn,* 'male'[72]

Key Scriptures: Genesis 1:27

Discernment:

- Paul: Placing hand on the right side of the body, a hit when I say, "male"
- Rob: Right side

MARRIAGE (61)

Category: Entity

History: First discerned early 2000s

Definition: Hebrew: *lāqaḥ,* 'take' (get, fetch), 'lay hold of' (seize), 'receive', 'acquire' (buy), 'bring', 'marry' (take a wife), 'snatch' (take away).[73] Greek: *gameo,* 'to marry'[74]

Key Scriptures: Genesis 2:23-24, 26:34; 1 Corinthians 7:10

Observations:

- Paul: In generational ministry, often has a husband repent for not spiritually covering the wives (protection) and then asks him to place his covering over his wife. Also has the wife repent for frustration over the husband not assuming his spiritual responsibility, which may have resulted in the her going into spiritual error by taking over the responsibly of spiritual direction for herself and her family.
- Barbara: When my husband prayed this, I sensed an umbrella open up above my head.

Discernment:

- Paul: Feel as a figure 8 on the husband and wife. When the husband is correctly covering the wife the top of the figure 8 goes over the wife. When the wife is in a position of submission to the protection of the husband the top of her figure eight goes through her husband's heart.

- Jana: Feels figure 8 over and around a couple facing each other

MAZZAROTH, OR ZODIAC (62)

Category: Being

History: First discerned, September 26, 2012; revelation regarding divine government on May 10, 2014; realized it is the righteous zodiac on September 5, 2016

Definition: Hebrew: *mazzārôt*, 'dubious'. Perhaps it refers to a particular star or constellation.[75] Greek: *kosmokrotoros*, A rare and late word, whose history is hard to follow. It is relatively common in astrological writings, where it means the planets, orig. perhaps as the rulers of the heavenly spheres, then as the rulers of the universe who also ordain the destinies of men.[76]

Key Scriptures: Job 38:32; Ephesians 6:12 (Rulers of darkness of this age)

Characteristics:

- Seems to be the executive branch of the divine government
- The word is in the plural and would indicate the twelve constellations (corruption of this is the zodiac in the various forms found in different nations). This would probably be related to the verse in Job 38:33 regarding the stars that "set their dominion over the earth"
- The twelve signs of the Mazzaroth are tied to the twelve tribes, the twelve stones on the High Priest ephod, and the twelve domains of the human body

Functions: Perhaps our assignments to rule over creations are connected to one or more of the twelve signs of the Mazzaroth

Discernment:

- Paul: Anointing all over the top of head, plus two points on the upper left side of head on either side of default evil spot

- Jana: Hears stars; feels slowly turning anointing on top of head
- Rob: Upper, left side of head
- Larry: Large anointing on and around head

MICHAEL (63)—SEE ALSO: ANGEL, ARCHANGEL

Category: Being

History: First discerned, 1996

Definition: Hebrew: *Mikael*, 'Who is like God?' Prince, *sar*, 'chieftain, chief, ruler, official, captain, prince' used 381 times in the Old Testament[77]

Key Scriptures: Daniel 10:10-13, 20-21; Daniel 12:1; Jude 9; Revelation 12:7-8

Characteristics: Described as a 'one of the great princes' to Daniel

Functions: Warrior; fought against Satan in the war in heaven; stands watch over Israel; contended with the devil over the body of Moses

Discernment:

- Paul: Overpowering force on the top left of head
- Jana: Right side of head, sometimes a movement as if traveling
- Rob: Top, right, middle part of head
- Larry: Powerful being and have to inquire what is present

MELCHIZEDEK (64)

Category: God

History:

- Mentioned at the formation of Joel's Well on September 22, 2008. A prophetic word was delivered, "A new awareness that I calling you to. Feed my sheep; protect my sheep. They are crying out; don't you hear them? They are desperate. If I do not have you, whom do I call on? Listen."
- First discerned May 23, 2010, on Pentecost, but was unaware of meaning until July, 2010

66

Definition: Hebrew: *malkî-ṣedeq*, Melchizedek[78] Greek: Melchizedek

Key Scriptures: Genesis 14:18, Psalm 110:4, Hebrews 5-7

Characteristics: Melchizedek is Jesus in His high priestly function as intercessor

Functions: Intercession

Observations: When discerned, wait for the end of the intercession and then discern the answer from the Father (per John 5:19)

Discernment:

- Paul: Effervescent sensation on left part of head (close to angel's spot)
- Jana: Sees robes; feels vibration
- Larry: Presence on side of head and inquires what is present

MERCY (SPIRITUAL GIFT) (65)

Category: Being

History: First discerned early 1990s

Definition: Greek: *eleeo*, 'to have mercy, to show kindness, by beneficence, or assistance', is translated 'have compassion' in Matthew 18:33 (KJV); Mark 5:19 and Jude 22[79]

Key Scriptures: Romans 12:8; Colossians 3:12

Discernment:

- Paul: Feels like a river that seems to have rapids flowing through the heart of a person, and can be discerned from far behind to far ahead of a person
- Jana: Feels like a river flowing from the heart

MORNING STAR (93)—SEE STARS

MT. ZION (66)

Category: Place

History: Early 2000's

Definition: Hebrew: *ṣîyôn*, 'Zion', Greek: *sion*, possibly related to Arabic *ṣâna*, 'protect', 'defend'; hence *ṣîyôn* may have meant 'place of defense', 'fortress'. Others suggest derivation from root *ṣâḥâ*, 'be bald'. Zion is the fortified mound between the Kidron and the Tyropean valleys that David captured from the Jebusites[80]

Key Scriptures: Psalm 48:2; Hebrews 12:22

Discernment:

- Paul: An anointing all over top of head and a hit saying, "Mt. Zion"

- Jana: Sees and feels a pyramid over the head

- Rob: Front-to-back sensation on entire head

- Larry: Power under my feet and have to inquire what is present

OLIVE TREES (67)

Category: Being

History: First discerned 2005

Definition: Hebrew: *zayit*, 'olive tree', 'olive'[81]

Key Scriptures: Zechariah 4; Revelation 11:4

Characteristics: The female tree is on the left and the male tree is on the right

Discernment:

- Paul: Feel the outline of the two trees with hand

- Jana: Sees trees

ORDER OF MELCHIZEDEK (68)—SEE ALSO: DOMAIN, REALM, WOMB OF THE DAWN, MELCHIZEDEK

Category: God, Place

History: Prophetic word, September 22, 2008; First discerned November 18, 2015

Definition: Hebrew: *debra*, 'cause', 'reason', 'manner'[82] Greek: 'an arranging, arrangement, order' (akin to *tasso*, 'to arrange, draw up in order')[83]

Key Scriptures: Psalm 110:4; Hebrews 7:11

Characteristics: A domain/realm

Functions: Place of intercession of our High Priest, Jesus Christ

Observations:

- During prayer, may be taken to the realm of the Order of Melchizedek to wait while Jesus' intercessions takes place, and then discern what the results are
- Seems to be involved in the formation of our spirits (as the sons of God) in the Womb of the Dawn
- We are not to be in the Levitical order, but in the Order of Melchizedek
- Seems to be tied to tribe of Levi and Pisces

Discernment:

- Paul: Top, back, left side of my head as two pressure points that often vibrate, one on the top and another just below it

- Jana: Sees a round platform with or without a grid

- Rob: Top, left side of head

- Larry: Feels a powerful expanse and have to inquire what is present

PALMONI, OR CERTAIN HOLY ONE (69)

Category: Being

History: First discerned, 2008

Definition: When Daniel was given a special prophecy by a certain holy one, this special messenger was called *palmoni*, which is annotated in the margin as the 'numberer of secrets', This appears to be a specialist which has to do with numbers. Numbers as well as words appear to hold a particular significant in the works of God.[84]

Key Scriptures: Daniel 8:13

Characteristics: Palmoni seems to vibrate at 444 HZ, which is the key of A above middle C. It may be the sound that was played at the dedication of Solomon's temple. (2 Chronicles 5:13-14)

Discernment:

- Paul: Vibration on head (like the library), plus ½ of the lower back of head

- Jana: Feels vibration in front of body between two pillars; feels with hand

- Rob: Feels vibration and inquires if it is Palmoni
- Larry: Vibration in front and inquires what is present

PASTOR (OFFICE) (70)

Category: Being

History: First discerned, early 2000s

Definition: Greek: *poimen*, 'a shepherd', one who tends herds or flocks used metaphorically of Christian pastors'[85]

Key Scriptures: Ephesians 4:11

Observations: This discernment can indicate either the office or function of Pastor, and may also indicate pastoring.

Discernment:

- Paul: Pressure on the ring finger of either the right or left hand. The right and left can indicate the mother's side (left) or the father's side (right). (Some believe left indicates what you are born with and right indicates what you should have faith for.)
- Jana: Pressure on second to last fingernail
- Rob: Pressure on left ring finger
- Larry: Pressure on ring finger, either hand

PATH(WAY) (71)

Category: Entity

History: Many prophetic words beginning in 2008; first discerned Winter 2016

Definition: Hebrew: *orah* is used in a figurative way, describing the way to life or to death. It often is parallel with the word *derek*, 'way', 'lifestyle'. "Teach me your way (*derek*), O Lord, and lead me in a plain (?) path (*'ōrah*)," (Psalm 27:11). "Do not enter the path (*'ōrah*) of the wicked, nor go in the way (*derek*) of evil men" (Proverbs 4:14; cf. Psalm 139:3; Proverbs 2:8, 12:28: Job 6:18; Isaiah 30:11).[86]

Key Scriptures: Psalm 16:11, 119:105, 142:3; Proverbs 15:19; Isaiah

35:8

Characteristics:

- These seem to be the highways of holiness Path
- Paul's life verse as a young man in the KJV was about being in the way the Lord led him
- Pathways appear to be inside of a grid line

Observations: Seems to be the walk of a person, which is established by that person. If a person's path is according to the Lord, then he/she is walking in the 'way' of the Lord.

Discernment:

- Paul: Like parallel bars on the top of my head ½ on the sides towards the front
- Jana: Sees and feels paths
- Rob: Like two train tracks on front of head
- Larry: Pathways under my feet and inquire what is present

PILLAR (72)

Category: Being

History: First discerned June 7, 2016

Definition: Hebrew: `ammûd, 'pillar', 'column'[87]

Key Scriptures: 1 Kings 7:21; Job 38:19; Proverbs 9; Jeremiah 1:10, 31:28

Characteristics:

- Dwelling of light
- Seven pillars of wisdom
- May also include other pillars, such as Boaz and Jachin
- Seem to look like cubes, but Paul feels as pillars
- Seem to be connected to a realm of supply—to new realms of supply
- Tied to mathematics (equations)
- Seem to be made of light
- Ungodly pillars seem to create a force field that separates segmenting in the brain. Limits thinking, causing confusing

- Ungodly pillars also may affect other organs—heart gall bladder, liver, etc.

Functions:

- Seem to uproot and tear down
- Seem to support the gates

Observations:

- Ungodly pillars seem to create a force field that separates and segments in the brain, limiting thinking and causing confusion.
- May also affect other organs—heart, gall bladder, liver, etc.

Discernment:

- Paul: Effervescent feeling on the back top of head on either side
- Jana: Sees vibrating translucent colors like a shaft of light; feels vibration
- Larry: Being in front of me and inquire what is present

PILLAR OF FIRE (3)—SEE ANGEL OF THE LORD AND FURNACE

POOL OF BETHESDA (73)
Category: Entity

History: First discerned 2016

Definition: Greek: *Bēthesdá*, 'lovingkindness', 'mercy'. Bethesda means house of mercy or flowing water. A pool in Jerusalem near the sheep gate or market with a building over or near it for the accommodation of the sick[88]

Key Scriptures: John 5:2

Discernment:

- Paul: An effervescent feeling (same as horses) all over the top of my head with a hit when I say, "Pool of Bethesda"
- Larry: Knowing in my spirit

POWER (74)
Category: Being

History: First discerned, 1994

Definition: Greek: *dynamis, dunamis* (doo'-nam-is), 'force' (literally or figuratively); especially, 'miraculous power' (usually by implication, a miracle itself)[89]; 'ability', 'abundance', 'might (-ily, -y, -y deed)', '(worker of) miracle (-s)', 'power', 'strength', 'violence', 'mighty' '(wonderful) work'[90]

Key Scriptures: Romans 8:38; Hebrews 6:5; 1 Peter 3:22

Characteristics: Associated with magnetic fields—see Appendix 3

Discernment:

- Paul: Back of the head

- Jana: Back of neck

- Larry: Back of the head

POWERS OF THE AGE TO COME (74)—SEE ALSO POWER
Category: Place

History: First discerned March 2, 2009; prophetic words 2010, 2015

Definition: Greek: *dunamis,* 'power'; ability, physical or moral, as residing in a person or thing[91] *aion,* 'an age, era'[92]

Key Scriptures: Hebrews 6:5

Observations: Word from Larry on April 23, 2015 Pearson, "...Take your seat in this realm; I am giving you a new power chariot with the Spirit of Elijah and fresh decrees; acceleration of manifestation and transformation unto a habitation for My Spirit upon the earth...Great authority is awakening, great power is coming...this is the hour where I shift My power to be triumphant by grace, to reveal the face of what was given before the foundations of the earth."

Discernment:

- Paul: Back of head (same as Powers)

- Jana: Word of knowledge and sense of presence of wisdom

- Larry: Overwhelming power and inquire what is present

PROPHET (OFFICE) (75)

Category: Being

History: First discerned, early 2000s

Definition: Hebrew: *nābî'*, 'spokesman', 'speaker', 'prophet' [93] Greek: *prophetes*, 'one who speaks forth or openly, a proclaimer of a divine message' [94]

Key Scriptures: Ephesians 4:11

Observations: Discernment can indicate either the office or function of the prophet, and can refer to prophecy.

Discernment:

- Paul: Pressure on index finger of either right or left hand.

- Jana: Feels river of anointing flowing through the eyes

- Rob: Pressure on index finger and inquires if office

- Larry: Pressure on index finger of either hand

PROPHET (SPIRITUAL GIFT) (76)

Category: Being

History: First discerned early 1990s

Definition: Greek: *propheteia*, signifies 'the speaking forth of the mind and counsel of God' [95]

Key Scriptures: Romans 12:6, 1 Corinthians. 14:1

Discernment:

- Paul: Like a river that seems to have rapids flowing through eyes of a person; discerned from far behind to far ahead

- Jana: Feels pressure on middle finger

- Rob: Pressure on index finger and inquires if spiritual gift

RADIANT GLORY (6)—SEE ARMOR OF LIGHT

RAINBOW ANGEL (77)—SEE ALSO ANGEL

Category: Being

History: First discerned, November 9, 2013

Definition: Greek: *iris* (like English word 'iris', the flower) describes the rainbow seen in the heavenly vision[96]

Key Scriptures: Revelation 10

Characteristics: The seven colors seem to be seven entries into dimensions.

Functions: The Rainbow angel carried a little book that seems to contain equations and information about DNA and RNA

Discernment:

- Paul: Arc on the center of head from right to left

- Jana: Sees rainbow; feels arch over head

- Rob: An arch overhead; also a sensation on left side of neck

- Larry: Great power and inquire what is present

REFINER'S FIRE (78)—SEE FURNACE

REFUGE (79)
Category: Being

History: First discerned, July 23, 2016

Definition: Hebrew: *ḥāsâ*, 'seek refuge'—flee for protection and thus figuratively put trust in (God), 'confide'—hope in (God or person)[97] Greek: *katapheúgō*, 'to flee'—to flee away to some place for refuge[98]

Key Scriptures: Psalm 7:1; Hebrew 6:18

Characteristics: This being is located beside the gate to the domain of refuge

Discernment:

- Paul: Same place as thrones and windows but effervescent, as two parallel bars on the ½ back part of head from front to back; also heavy pressure where I feel angels

- Jana: Sees a large wing

- Larry: A lot of heat in my belly and have to inquire what is present

RIVER OF GOD (25)

Category: Entity

History: First discerned, March 3, 2017

Definition: Hebrew: *nāhār*, 'river' [99] Greek: *potamos*, 'a river, stream, torrent' [100]

Key Scriptures: Genesis 2:10; Ezekiel 47:5-12; Revelation 21:1-2

Discernment:

- Paul: Feels it flowing across the middle of the head from right to left

- Jana: Feels a flow around the legs and confirms by feeling with hand

ROOTS (80)

Category: Entity

History: First discerned, 2015

Definition: Hebrew: *sores*, 'root'—used mostly in a figurative sense in the Old Testament. It serves as a natural figure for the lower parts or foundations of something. [101]
Greek: *rhizoo* "to cause to take root," is used metaphorically in the passive voice in Eph. 3:17, of being "rooted" in love [102]

Key Scriptures: Psalm 1; Proverbs 12:3; Colossians 2:7

Characteristics: Seem to be the foundational structure of body, soul and spirit

Discernment:

- Paul: Strong pulling sensation on bottom of feet, often including a cramping sensation in feet

- Jana: Sees roots

- Rob: Underneath feet

RULER (81)

Category: Being

History: First discerned, 2008

Definition: Greek: *archon*, always signifies 'primacy' whether in time: 'beginning' or *principium*; or in

rank: 'power', 'dominion', 'office', 'supernatural power'. (Some versions translate as 'principalities' though the concept does not seem to be supported by scripture)

Key Scriptures: 1 Corinthians 2:6; Ephesians 3:10, 6:12; Colossians 1:16

Characteristics: Sits at the table of showbread

Observations: Psalm 23 seems to be about the rulers

Discernment:

- Paul: Back of head by neck (same as powers)
- Jana: Feels power at back, middle of head and neck
- Rob: Back of head
- Larry: Power on back of head and inquire what is present

SCRIBE (83)

Category: Being

History: First discerned, September 16, 2015, when the Library was felt, and realized on November 23, 2016, that what was initially thought to be the librarian was actually a scribe, who not only recorded but also wrote and managed scrolls and books.

Definition: Hebrew: *sopher*, 'scribe', 'learned' [103] Greek: *grammateus*, 'a scribe', 'a man of letters', 'a teacher of the law' [104]

Key Scriptures: 2 Samuel 20:25; Ezra 4:9; Matthew 13:52

Observations: Write down everything that is said and done

Discernment:

- Paul: Top ½ front of my head
- Jana: Sees a writing box and quill; word of knowledge in the library
- Larry: Sees a pen

SCROLL (SEE BOOK) (9)—SEE ALSO: LAW

SELAH (84)—SEE ALSO: KAIROS AND PALMONI

Category: Entity, place

History: Discerned August 28, 2015; increased revelation began January 13, 2016

Definition: Hebrew: *selah,* a musical notation, perhaps designating a pause in performance, occurring over 70 times in psalm texts[105]

Key Scriptures: Psalm 3:2, 24:10; Habakkuk 3:3, 9, 13

Characteristics: Feels like a pause; very quiet, as if nothing is happening; palmoni is in this place; may be located in the womb of the Dawn; a way to time and dimensions and seems to be the only way to certain heavenly places

Functions:
- Way of escape
- Sound of thinking to heal or destroy
- Carries one to a place of inheritance

Discernment:
- Paul: Effervescence on top middle of head from side to side
- Jana: Word of knowledge

SERAPHIM (85)

Category: Being

History: First discerned, early 2000s

Definition: Hebrew: *saraf,* 'seraph' literally means 'burning one', perhaps suggesting that these creatures had a fiery appearance. Elsewhere in the OT seraph refers to poisonous snakes (Numbers 21:6; Deuteronomy 8:15; Isaiah 14:29; 30:6). Perhaps they were called burning ones because of their appearance or the effect of their venomous bites, which would cause a victim to burn up with fever. It is possible that the seraphs seen by Isaiah were at least partially serpentine in appearance. Though it might seem strange for a snake-like creature to have wings, two of the texts where seraphs are snakes describe them as 'flying' (Isaiah 14:29; 30:6), perhaps referring to their darting movements.[106]

Key Scriptures: Isaiah 6:1-8

Characteristics: Worship

Observations: "…seraphs, each with six wings: With two wings they covered their faces, with two they covered their feet, and with two they were flying. And they were calling to one another: "Holy, holy, holy is the LORD Almighty; the whole earth is full of his glory." At the sound of their voices the doorposts and thresholds shook and the temple was filled with smoke." (From Isaiah passage)

Discernment:

- Paul: Effervescent feeling (senses this is the fire coming up from the feet)

- Jana: Sees thin being; feels fire coming up from feet

- Rob: Feels like burning fire over mouth

- Rob: Left top of head; may sense coals of fire being placed on the mouth

SEVEN EYES OF THE LORD (SEE APPENDIX 4)—SEE SEVEN SPIRITS OF GOD

Discernment:
Paul: Feels each eye with hand

SEVEN SPIRITS OF GOD (86)

Category: Being, entity, place

History: First discerned, 2006

Definition: Identified as the Spirit of the Lord and of wisdom, understanding, counsel, might, knowledge, and fear of the Lord

Key Scriptures: Isaiah 11:1-2; Zechariah 3:9, 4:10; Revelation 5:6

Characteristics: Located at the candlestick in the tabernacle; also around the throne of God

Functions: Sent out into all the earth

Observations: Tied to the seven eyes of the Lord, which are discerned on the body, and seem to be what those outside of Christianity call chakra points; may appear individually or all at once

Discernment:

- Paul: Sudden increase in temperature that feels like a hot flash
- Jana: Senses them in a circle and tests by feeling each one with hands
- Rob: Burning sensation on right
- Larry: Burning up the back and inquire what is present

SEVEN THUNDERS (87)

Category: Being

History: First discerned, 2016

Definition: Hebrew: *bronte*, 'thunder', 'thunders'

Key Scriptures: Revelation 10:3-4

Characteristics: Seem to carry end time prophetic words

Discernment:

- Paul: Two parallel bars on the left and right hand side of the top of my head from the middle of my head to the back—same as pillars

SHIELD OF FAITH (88)—SEE ALSO: FAITH

Category: Entity

History: First discerned, April 17, 2016

Definition: Greek: *thureos*, formerly meant 'a stone for closing the entrance of a cave'; then, 'a shield', large and oblong, protecting every part of the soldier; the word is used metaphorically of faith.[107]

Key Scriptures: Ephesians 6:16

Discernment:

- Paul: Like many feelers coming off back of head with sense of something that looks like a sea anemone; also feels like a force field
- Jana: Feels a shield in front of her

SILVER CORD (89)

Category: Entity

History: First discerned very early, probably around 2000

Definition: Hebrew: *kesep*, silver as in metal; *hebel*, 'cord', 'rope' [108]

Key Scriptures: Ecclesiastes 12:6

Characteristics: The silver cord is tied to what psychologist call bonding. The silver cord is attached to mother and father.

Observations:

- Paul: Once prayed for a small child who would never let his mother hold him and found that his silver cord was not attached to his mother (i.e. for some reason never bonded with his mother). The mother asked that his silver cord would be attached to her. She called later and related that her son climbed into her lap and remained there for over 2 hours.

- Paul: Has noticed that husbands and wives often try to hold onto their spouse's silver cord, attempting to draw life from them (i.e. have the spouse meet their needs). There have been dramatic results when a spouse repents and releases his/her spouse's silver cord back to the Lord.

- Sometimes Paul feels cord dangling, which means child not attached to parents; may have parent pick up cord; often occurs when child was not wanted at first

Discernment:

- Paul: Feel the cord coming off of a person's belly button.

- Jana: Sees a silver cord

- Larry: Sense a cord in front of me or others

SON OF MAN (90)

Category: God

History: First discerned February 2013

Definition: Greek: *huios*, 'a son' [109] Also, *anthropos*, used of 'a human being, male or female', without reference to sex or nationality[110]

Key Scriptures: Daniel 7:13; Matthew 12:8; Mark 14:62

Discernment:

- Paul: Left side of head just below stars

- Jana: Left side of body, like human but holy

- Larry: Left side of head and inquire what is present

SON(S) OF GOD (91)

Category: Being

History: First discerned, 2011

Definition: *Bene ha elohim*, 'sons of God' [111]

Key Scriptures: Genesis 6:1-2; Judges 5:8; 1 Samuel 28:13-14; Job 1:6-7; Luke 3:38; Romans 8:19

Characteristics:

- May be righteous or unrighteous; revealed or fallen
- Sexual relationships of fallen sons with daughters of men resulted in the Nephilim and the Rephaim
- Fallen sons represent the mythological pantheons of various cultures

Discernment:

- Paul: Side of head

- Jana: Effervescence on left side, especially back of shoulder

- Larry: Left side of my head and have to inquire what is present

SPIRITUAL GIFTS—SEE EXHORTATION, GIVING, HEALING, LEADER, MERCY, PROPHET, TEACHER

SPIRITUAL FORCES (92)

Category: Being

History: First discerned, 2017

Definition: Greek: *pneumatikov,* can be translated as wind, breath, life, soul, spirit, spirit of the dead, conjurer up of spirits of the dead, the deceased in the grave; of wickedness; *ponerias,* defectiveness, physical sickness in both animals and men; it is the intentionally practiced evil; in Hebrew the word means poor and useless state, badness of fruits, the ugliness and unprepossessing nature of animal, bad mood, sorrowful mien, displeasure, misfortune, evil, days of disaster, bad, troubled situation evil men do to one another, hence in the sense of injury and also expression of an evil disposition evil plan or purpose, maliciousness, evil individual wicked acts, wickedness of the wicked, haughtiness, violence, and hardness of heart.

Key Scriptures: Ephesians 6:12

Observations:

- Appear to be inter-dimensional
- Per Dr. Tom Hawkins, "The word 'forces' is added because in English the idea is incomplete. The translation 'spiritual evil' is used because in the context they would seem to be some kind of 'power' or 'force' with personality, not just a cosmological 'evil' that somehow permeates the world."

Discernment:

- Paul: Top ½ back of head as radiating power going up (same as books)
- Jana: Anointing on back of head that radiates up

STAR (93)—SEE ALSO: MAZZAROTH, HOST

Category: Being

History: First discerned May 3, 2009

Definition: Hebrew: *kôkāb*, 'star', Greek: *aster*, 'a star' [112]

Key Scriptures: Judges 5:20; Job 22:12, 38:7; Psalm 148:3; Isaiah 14:12–13; Amos 5:26; 2 Peter 1:19; Revelation 2:28

Characteristics:

- Discernment is of spiritual stars, not physical stars
- There are righteous and unrighteous stars.
- Human's spirit parts can be attached (stuck) in ungodly stars, star systems, zodiacs, constellation and galaxies
- Powerful
- Somehow tied or assigned to man

Functions:

- Warfare
- Righteous ones praise God
- Jesus is THE morning star, but we can also have morning stars assigned to us

Observations:

- Sometimes personalized

- May be identified with the sons of God who sang forth praise at the creation
- Through discernment they seem to be positioned at the Ark of the Covenant
- It seems possible that the enemy wanted to exalt himself in power above the stars because they are very powerful

Discernment:

- Paul: Top left part of head
- Jana: Hears sound; sees sparkles
- Rob: Hears high pitched screeching; may feel anywhere on body as hot, fiery sensation
- Larry: Hear sounds

SUN OF RIGHTEOUSNESS (94)
Category: Being

History: First time Paul discerned the Sun of Righteousness he could tell that a huge angel, at least 40 feet high, was present and that it had an anointing of healing

Definition: Hebrew: *šemeš*, 'sun'[113] *ṣĕdāqâ*, 'justice', 'righteousness'[114]

Key Scriptures: Malachi 4:2

Characteristics:

- Hebrew words in Malachi 4:2 are feminine, not masculine
- Appears to be female; associated with healing

Discernment:

- Paul: Upper part of my hand (same as healing), and an effervescence on the left side of my head where angels and seraphim are discerned
- Jana: Feels wings on both sides of body
- Rob: Heat and pressure across hands, below fingers

TEACHER (OFFICE) (95)
Category: Being

History: First discerned, early 2000s

Definition: Hebrew: *moreh*, 'a teacher' [115] Greek: *didaskalos*, 'a teacher' [116]

Key Scriptures: Ephesians 4:11

Observations: Discernment can refer to either the office or the function of Teacher, and may indicate teaching

Discernment:

- Paul: Little finger of either my right or left hand
- Jana: Pressure on little finger
- Rob: Pressure on little finger
- Larry: Pressure on little finger left or right

TEACHER (SPIRITUAL GIFT) (96)

Category: Being

History: First discerned early 1990s

Definition: Greek: *didasko*, 'to give instruction' [117]

Key Scriptures: Romans 12:7; Matthew 28:20

Discernment:

- Paul: Like a river that seems to have rapids flowing through the brain of a person, discerned from far behind to far ahead
- Jana: Feels like river flowing off of head

THRONE (97)—SEE ALSO: RAINBOW ANGEL, SEVEN THUNDERS, HEIGHT

Category: Being

History: First discerned, September 20, 2015

Definition: Greek: *Thronos*, 'a throne', 'a seat of authority' [118]

Key Scriptures: Colossians 1:16

Characteristics:

- Very large beings, perhaps larger than the cherubim
- Do not appear to be thrones we sit on, but rather are thrones that are aligned with us

- Seem to be tied to the most, if not all, beings
- The seven thunders seem to be located under the thrones
- Tied to ruling and reigning in the height
- Seem connected by sound to the thrones of God
- Seem to have a connection with healing
- Seem to be located in the place of the rest of the Lord
- Tied to wealth
- May activate gifts
- Seem to be the power source under the Trinity for many spiritual beings and activities
- There's a top echelon that appears to be the main operators that control the power flow to other thrones and other spiritual beings

Functions: Release the powerful presence of the Lord

Observations:

- It appears that our spiritual gifts, anointings, callings need to be plugged into thrones in order to function, in which case what we call 'activation' may be when our giftings are plugged in to the thrones
- Also may be how evil uses our God-given gifts/anointings/callings either by plugging them or having us plug them into fallen thrones.

Discernment:

- Paul: Top of head on both sides, like parallel bars from center to the back
- Jana: Pressure on both sides of top of head
- Rob: Pressure on middle, top of head
- Larry: Great power and inquire what is present

THUMMIN (101)—SEE URIM AND THUMMIN

TONGUES (OF MAN) (98)
Category: Being
History: First discerned with hands, 1994; First discerned on head,

March 21, 2015

Definition: Greek, *glossa*, (a) 'a language' coupled with *phule*, 'a tribe', *laos*, 'a people', *ethnos*, 'a nation', (b) 'the supernatural gift of speaking in another language without its having been learnt' [119]

Key Scriptures: Psalm 104:4; Acts 2:3; I Corinthians 13:1, 14:2-27; Hebrew 1:7

Characteristics:

- There are tongues that are earthly languages that have not been learned by an individual as well as unique tongues that are angelic languages
- Appears like a flame of fire

Functions: Deliver a message directly from the Lord to an individual

Observations: A tongue of angels is much different than tongues of men in that the tongues is often made up of unusual sounds and tones.

Discernment:

- Paul: Left side of head close to where Holy Spirit is felt and get a hit by saying, "tongue of man" or "tongue of fire"

- Jana: Sees a tongue of fire; word of knowledge

- Larry: Top of head and inquire what is present, kowing in my spirit

TONGUES OF ANGELS (99)—SEE ALSO: TONGUES

Category: Being

History: First discerned March 21, 2015

Definition: Greek: *glossa*, the 'tongues ... like as of fire' which appeared at Pentecost, Greek: *angelos*, 'a messenger' [120]

Key Scriptures: 1 Corinthians 13:1, 14:2-27

Characteristics: Appear as a tongue of fire

Observations: A tongue of angels is much different than tongues of men in that the tongues is often made up of unusual sounds and tones

Discernment:

- Paul: Left side of head close to where Holy Spirit is felt and get a hit by saying, "tongue of angels"

- Jana: Hears singing of musical scales

- Larry: Knowing in my spirit

TREE OF LIFE (74)—SEE POWER

TRUTH (100)
Category: Being

History: First discerned, July 3, 2016

Definition: Hebrew: *emet,* at the heart of the meaning of the root is the idea of certainty and this is borne out by the NT definition of faith found in Heb 11:1[121]; Greek: *aletheia,* 'truth', is used objectively, signifying 'the reality lying at the basis of an appearance; the manifested, veritable essence of a matter' [122]

Key Scriptures: Psalm 108:4; John 8:32

Discernment:

- Paul: Pressure point just right of where the Son of Man is felt, and just above righteousness and justice

- Rob: Slightly above left ear

- Larry: Knowing in my spirit

URIM AND THUMMIN (101)
Category: Entity

History: First discerned, May 2014

Definition: *Urim* and *Thummim* are two un-translated Hebrew words that might mean 'lights and perfections'. They refer to some kind of stones or tokens that the ancient high priests of Israel used for discovering the will of God [123]

Key Scriptures: Exodus 28:30,

Characteristics: The Urim and Thummim were used in connection with the breastplate of judgment worn by the high priest in ancient Israel, and were placed in the breastplate, perhaps in a bag or pouch

Functions: To determine the will of the Lord

Observations: Authors now believe that the high priests could discern a yes or no answer with their hand, by placing it over Urim or Thummin, and in this way they would inquire of the Lord

Discernment:

- Paul: Felt on chest, with Urim on left and Thummin on right; a hit on the left indicates answer from the Lord is yes, and a hit on right means no

- Jana: Feels Urim on right chest and Thummin on left chest

- Rob: Feels Urim on right and Thummin on left

- Larry: Same as Paul

VOICE OF MANY WATERS (102)

Category: God

History: First discerned, early 2016

Definition: Hebrew: Greek: *phone*, most frequently 'a voice'; may be translated 'sound'[124]

Key Scriptures: Ezekiel 1:24, 43:2; Revelation 1:15, 14:2, 19:6

Discernment:

- Paul: Back of head where powers are felt, and get a hit when saying, "voice of many waters"

- Jana: Hear what sounds like a trillion voices at the same time

WALLS (34)—SEE DOMINION

WATCHER (103)

Category: Being

History: First discerned May 6, 2012

Definition: Hebrew: *'ir*, 'waking', 'watchful' [125]

Key Scriptures: Job 13:27; Song of Solomon 5:7; Daniel 4:13,17, 8:13

Characteristics:

- Stand on the walls, so they may stand on the grid lines; may be righteous or unrighteous
- Appear to be like sentinels
- Seem to be the enforcement arm of the judicial branch (like marshals)
- Extremely huge beings that appear humanoid

Functions:

- Report time; righteous guard over the harvest, so ungodly ones would block evangelism; righteous protect from evil, and ungodly allow destruction from within; a kind of holy one; seem to be over the cellular level

Observations:

- Seers report that righteous watchers look more like soldiers and ungodly watchers look like corrupt politicians
- Often called sentinels or guardians by those who see them
- Many who look at the book of Enoch believe that watchers are the same as the sons of God and the same as angels, but the authors believe watchers are a total unique spiritual being

Discernment:

- Paul: Feels strong burning sensation all over back of head
- Rob: Back of head
- Larry: Sees peering eyes in spirit and inquire what is present

WAY (71)—SEE PATHWAY

WHIRLWIND (104)

Category: Entity

History: First prophetic words on March 14, 2005; first discerned October 17, 2014, Kaneohe, Hawaii

Definition: Hebrew: *searah*, 'tempest', 'storm wind' [126], *saar*, 'to sweep or whirl away', 'storm', 'sweep them away', 'tempestuous', 'whirls him away'[127] *suphah*, 'storm wind', 'gale', 'storm', 'tempest', 'whirlwind', 'windstorms' [128] Greek: *thuella*, 'hurricane', 'cyclone', 'whirlwind' [129]

Key Scriptures: 2 Kings 2:1-11; Job 38:1; Proverbs 1:27; Isaiah 29:6; Hosea 8:7; Nahum 1:3; Hebrews 12:18

Discernment:

- Paul: Circular motion on head in a going from right to left; also feel around me by putting my hand out in front

- Jana: Sees and feels whirlwind

- Rob: Feels a whirlwind above head

- Larry: Sees and feels whirlwinds

WIDTH (105)

Category: Entity, Being

History: First discerned, July 12, 2010

Definition: Greek: *plátos*, 'broad breadth', figuratively, the great expanses of the earth, the width [130]

Key Scriptures: Ephesians 3:18

Characteristics: The place of faith, hope and love; fallen width would contain despair; place of the heart

Observations: Has been observed as a massive being

Discernment:

- Paul: Like a wall circling the top of my head, but most often get a word of knowledge rather than discernment

- Jana: Feels with hand

- Rob: Feels dimensional shifting and inquires where

- Tobias: Sees army-green color, as if on a graph but with much more substance than a line

WINDOW(S) (106)

Category: Entity

History: First thought of them on my birthday after a dream about on January 12, 2015; first discerned February 23, 2016

Definition: Hebrew: *ărŭbâ,* (ʾărŭbâ), 'window', 'chimney', 'floodgate'. Twice the word is used to describe one of the two sources of the waters in the deluge (Gen 7:11; 8:2). In addition to rain from above there was also an auxiliary source, 'the fountains of the great deeps', i.e. subterranean water. The phrase 'windows of heaven', in the deluge context, is in some of the more recent Bible translations rendered 'sluices', (NIV 'floodgates'). There is no reason not to believe that the writer in Genesis when using the phrase 'window of heavens' was well aware of his own figurative language to describe the torrential downpour. If God channels the waters of judgment and cleansing through these windows, he also sends his blessing through these same windows (Mal 3:10). Similarly compare II Kgs 7:2, 19 where Elisha has made predictions of an incredible reduction in the price of food, much to the disbelief of the king's squire. Thus, such apertures are the means of God's cleansing or his blessing. Two unique uses of 'ărūbâ are (1) window, in the sense of a 'chimney' through which smoke passes (Hos 3:13), and (2) the small opening in a pigeon loft (Isa 60:8). The reference to 'those who look out of windows are darkened' (Eccl 12:3) is probably not a poetical reference to the eyes which become dim with old age, but to some funereal practice (Dahood), or some disaster of unidentifiable nature (Sawyer).[131]

Key Scriptures: 2 Kings 7:2, 7:19; Song of Songs 2:9; Joel 2:9; Malachi 3:10

Characteristics: Seem to have branches that come through and connect to the person and the gates and doors on the grid; same place as thrones

Observations:
- Female window(s) seem to be on left side of body; male window(s) on right side
- Seem to become active at sundown
- Note from June 6, 2014: Song of Songs 2:9, "Gazing through the window, peering through the lattice." Windows and lattices are different from doors.

Discernment:
- Paul: Two parallel bars on the two sides of my head, beginning ½ the way back to the back of my head
- Jana: Sees a window in a frame

- Larry: Sees a window in his spirit

WISDOM (107)
Category: Being

History: First discerned, December, 2016

Definition: Hebrew: *chokmah,* 'wisdom' [132]

Key Scriptures: Proverbs 8, 9

Discernment:

- Paul: Parallel bars across lower back; also parallel bars on back, top ½ of head

- Jana: Word of knowledge; sees powers of the age to come

- Rob: On chin, like a beard

- Larry: Knowing in my spirit and inquire what is present

WOMB OF THE DAWN (108)
Category: Entity

History: First discerned, February 25, 2015

Definition: Hebrew: *rechem,* 'womb' 21 times, and 'matrix' five times;[133] Greek: *mišhār,* 'dawn' [134]

Key Scriptures: Psalm 110:3

Characteristics: Seems to be the place where the spirits known as the sons of god are formed in the realm of Melchizedek

Discernment:

- Paul: Like a ledge on forehead.

- Jana: Sees sunset over water

- Rob: Sensation like a visor coming off front of head

- Larry: Word of knowledge

WORD OF LIFE (109)
Category: God

History: First discerned, 1/28/2017

Definition: Greek: *logos,* 'a word or saying', also means 'an account which one gives by word of mouth'[135] *zoe*, (Eng., "zoo," "zoology") is used in the NT 'of life as a principle', 'life in the absolute sense', 'life as God has it' [136]

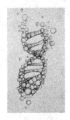

Key Scriptures: Philippians 2:16; 1 John 1:1, Hebrews 4:12

Discernment:

- Paul: Effervescent sensation on left side of head beginning on top of neck and going up to top left side of head

- Larry: Sees a book opened in the Spirit

ZODIAC (62)—SEE MAZZAROTH

[1] Harris, R. L., Archer, G. L., Jr., & Waltke, B. K. (Eds.). (1999). *Theological Wordbook of the Old Testament* (electronic ed., p. 1056). Chicago: Moody Press.

[2] http://biblehub.net/searchstrongs.php?q=angel

[3] Strong, J. (1995). *Enhanced Strong's Lexicon*. Woodside Bible Fellowship.

[4] Vine, W. E., Unger, M. F., & White, W., Jr. (1996). *Vine's Complete Expository Dictionary of Old and New Testament Words* (Vol. 2, p. 30). Nashville, TN: T. Nelson.

[5] http://biblehub.com/greek/743.htm

[6] Vine, Unger & White, 37-38.

[7] Ibid., p. 79.

[8] Ibid., p. 369.

[9] http://biblehub.com/greek/1849.htm

[10] *Greek-English Lexicon* by Ardnt and Gingrich

[11] *Dictionary of New Testament Theology*

[12] http://www.merriam-webster.com/dictionary/authority

[13] Vine, Unger & White, 45.

[14] Ibid.

[15] Kaiser, W. C. (1999). 1928 צָמַח. R. L. Harris, G. L. Archer Jr., & B. K. Waltke (Eds.), *Theological Wordbook of the Old Testament* (electronic ed., p. 769). Chicago: Moody Press.

[16] Kittel, G., Bromiley, G. W., & Friedrich, G. (Eds.). (1964–). *Theological dictionary of the New Testament* (electronic ed., Vol. 3, p. 757). Grand Rapids, MI: Eerdmans.

[17] Mccomiskey, T. E. (1999). 83 אִישׁ. R. L. Harris, G. L. Archer Jr., & B. K. Waltke (Eds.), *Theological Wordbook of the Old Testament* (electronic ed., p. 38). Chicago: Moody Press.

[18] Alden, R. (1999). 1349 נחשׁ. R. L. Harris, G. L. Archer Jr., & B. K. Waltke (Eds.), *Theological Wordbook of the Old Testament* (electronic ed., p. 572). Chicago: Moody Press.

[19] Cohen, G. G. (1999). 2295 רָשָׁר. R. L. Harris, G. L. Archer Jr., & B. K. Waltke (Eds.), *Theological Wordbook of the Old Testament* (electronic ed., p. 884). Chicago: Moody Press.

[20] Hartley, J. E. (1999). 1865 צָבָא. R. L. Harris, G. L. Archer Jr., & B. K. Waltke (Eds.), *Theological Wordbook of the Old Testament* (electronic ed., p. 750). Chicago: Moody Press.

[21] Strong.

[22] http://biblehub.com/hebrew/3742.htm

[23] Vine, Unger & White, 107.

[24] Ibid., p. 680.

[25] Vine, Unger, & White, 218.

[26] Ibid., 154.

[27] Ibid.

[28] Ibid.

[29] http://www.merriam-webster.com/dictionary/grid

[30] *American Heritage Talking Dictionary.* Copyright 1997. The Learning Company, Inc.

[31] Hamilton, V. P. (1999). 431 דָּלָה. R. L. Harris, G. L. Archer Jr., & B. K. Waltke (Eds.), *Theological Wordbook of the Old Testament* (electronic ed., p. 189). Chicago: Moody Press.

[32] Vine, Unger & White, Vol. 2, p. 180.

[33] Strong.

[34] Strong.

[35] *Vines Expository Dictionary* Copyright (C) 1985, Thomas Nelson Publishers

[36] Strong.

[37] Vine, Unger, & White, 19.

[38] Ibid., 208.

[39] Ibid., 110.

[40] Ibid., 2.

[41] Zodhiates, S. (2000). *The complete word study dictionary: New Testament* (electronic ed.). Chattanooga, TN: AMG Publishers.

[42] Strong

[43] Youngblood, R. F. (1999). 2526 תַּנּוּר. R. L. Harris, G. L. Archer Jr., & B. K. Waltke (Eds.), *Theological Wordbook of the Old Testament* (electronic ed., p. 974). Chicago: Moody Press.

[44] Hartley, 777.

[45] Strong.

[46] http://biblehub.com/hebrew/1403.htm

[47] http://www.biblestudytools.com/dictionary/gabriel/

[48] Austel, H. J. (1999). 2437 שׁער. R. L. Harris, G. L. Archer Jr., & B. K. Waltke (Eds.), *Theological Wordbook of the Old Testament* (electronic ed., p. 945). Chicago: Moody Press.

[49] Vine, Unger & White, 261.

[50] Elwell, W. A., & Comfort, P. W. (2001). In *Tyndale Bible Dictionary*. Wheaton, IL: Tyndale House Publishers.

[51] Zodhiates

[52] Vine, Unger, & White

[53] Thomas, R. L. (1998). *New American Standard Hebrew-Aramaic and Greek dictionaries : updated edition*. Anaheim: Foundation Publications, Inc.

[54] Vine, Unger, & White, 169.

[55] http://biblehub.com/hebrew/2091.htm

[56] http://biblehub.com/hebrew/1543.htm

[57] Vine, Unger & White, 295.

[58] Zodhiates

[59] Wolf, H. (1999). 453 דָּרַךְ. R. L. Harris, G. L. Archer Jr., & B. K. Waltke (Eds.), *Theological Wordbook of the Old Testament* (electronic ed., p. 196). Chicago: Moody Press.

[60] Mccomiskey, 786.

[61] http://biblehub.com/hebrew/1706.htm

[62] Harris, Archer, & Waltke

[63] Vine, Unger & White, Vol. 2, p. 449.

[64] Strong,.

[65] Vine, Unger & White, Vol. 2, p. 354.

[66] Ibid., Vol. 2, p. 386.

[67] Zodhiates

[68] Vine, Unger & White, Vol. 2, p. 371.

[69] Zodhiates

[70] Vine, Unger & White, Vol. 2, p. 374.

[71] www.Dictionary.com

[72] Thomas

[73] Kaiser, Harris, Archer & Waltke

[74] Vine, Unger & White, Vol. 2, p. 394.

[75] Harris, Archer & Waltke, 498.

[76] Kittel, Bromiley, & Friedrich, 913. It is the authors' opinion that Kosmokratoros is the same as the Mazzaroth.

[77] http://biblehub.com/hebrew/8269.htm

[78] Culver, R. D. (1999). 1199 מָלַךְ. R. L. Harris, G. L. Archer Jr., & B. K. Waltke (Eds.), *Theological Wordbook of the Old Testament* (electronic ed., p. 507). Chicago: Moody Press.

[79] Vine, Unger & White, Vol. 2, 117.

[80] Hartley, 764.

[81] Vine, Unger & White, Vol. 2, 450.

[82] Kalland, E. S. (1999). 399 דָּבַר. R. L. Harris, G. L. Archer Jr., & B. K. Waltke (Eds.), *Theological Wordbook of the Old Testament* (electronic ed.). Chicago: Moody Press.

[83] Vine, Unger & White, Vol. 2, 450.

[84] *Cosmic Codes*, Chuck Missler, p. 281.

[85] Vine, Unger & White, Vol. 2, 462.

[86] Hamilton, 71.

[87] Allen, R. B. (1999). 1637 עָמַד. R. L. Harris, G. L. Archer Jr., & B. K. Waltke (Eds.), *Theological Wordbook of the Old Testament* (electronic ed., p. 673). Chicago: Moody Press.

[88] Zodhiates

[89] Strong

[90] KJV

[91] Vine, Unger & White, Vol. 2, 2.

[92] Ibid., 19.

[93] Culver, 544

[94] Vine, Unger & White, Vol. 2, 493.

[95] Ibid., 492.

[96] Ibid., 505.

[97] Wiseman, D. J. (1999). 700 חָסָה. R. L. Harris, G. L. Archer Jr., & B. K. Waltke (Eds.), *Theological Wordbook of the Old Testament* (electronic ed., p. 307). Chicago: Moody Press.

[98] Zodhiates

[99] Harris

[100] Vine, Unger & White, Vol. 2, 243.

[101] Austel, 957.

[102] Vine, Unger & White, Vol. 2, 539.

[103] Thomas

[104] Vine, Unger & White, Vol. 2, 551.

[105] Elwell & Comfort.

[106] (Biblical Studies Press. (2006). *The NET Bible First Edition Notes* (Is 6:2). Biblical Studies Press}

[107] Vine, Unger & White, Vol. 2, 571.

[108] Weber, C. P. (1999). 592 חָבַל. R. L. Harris, G. L. Archer Jr., & B. K. Waltke (Eds.), *Theological Wordbook of the Old Testament* (electronic ed., p. 258). Chicago: Moody Press.

[109] Vine, Unger & White, Vol. 2, 99.

[110] Ibid., 388.

[111] https://en.wikipedia.org/wiki/Sons_of_God

[112] Vine, Unger & White, 180.

[113] Hartley, 940.

[114] Stigers, H. G. (1999). 1879 צָדַק. R. L. Harris, G. L. Archer Jr., & B. K. Waltke (Eds.), *Theological Wordbook of the Old Testament* (electronic ed., p. 752). Chicago: Moody Press.

[115] Thomas

[116] Vine, Unger & White, 180.

[117] Ibid., 619.

[118] Ibid., 631.

[119] Ibid., 636.

[120] Ibid., 26.

[121] Scott, J. B. (1999). 116 אָמַן. R. L. Harris, G. L. Archer Jr., & B. K. Waltke (Eds.), *Theological Wordbook of the Old Testament* (electronic ed., p. 51). Chicago: Moody Press.

[122] Vine, Unger & White, 645.

[123] Elwell & Comfort

[124] Vine, Unger & White, 589.

[125] Ibid.

[126] Thomas

[127] Ibid.

[128] Ibid.

[129] Vine, Unger & White, 621.

[130] Zodhiates

[131] Hamilton, 68–69.

[132] Strong

[133] Strong

[134] Hamilton, 917.

[135] Vine, Unger & White, 10.

[136] Ibid., 367.

DISCERNMENT MAPPING

KEY:

1	Ancient of Days	25	Burning Bush, Eternity, I AM, River of God
2	Angel		
3	Angel of the Lord, Pillar of Fire	26	Evangelist (Office)
4	Ancient Path	27	Lion of Judah
5	Apostle (Office)	28	Exhortation, Encouragement
5a	Archangel	29	Father as Power
6	Armor of Light, Radient Glory	30	Femaleness
		31	Fiery Stones
7	Authorities	32	Furnace
8	Authority	33	Gabriel
9	Book, Scroll	34	Dominion, Wall
10	Branch	35	Gatekeeper, Doorkeeper
11	Breakthrough Angel/Anointing	36	Giving
12	Bronze Man	37	Glorious Ones
13	Captain/Commander of the Host	38	Glory of God, Horns
14	Chariots of Fire	39	Golden Bowl
15	Cherub(im)	40	Golden Pipes
16	Chromosome	41	Glory Realm
17	Cloud	42	Healing
18	Cloud of Witnesses	43	Height
19	Council of the Lord	44	Highways of Holiness, Ley Lines
20	Deep	45	Holiness
21	Depth	46	Holy Spirit
22	Door, Gate	47	Honey
23	Elder	48	Horse
24	Elemental Spirits	49	Host

FRONT OF PAUL'S HEAD

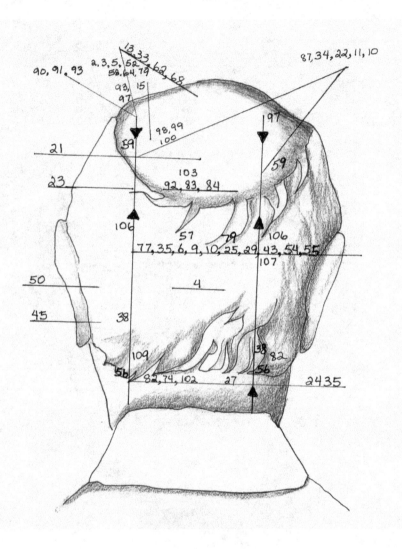

TOP OF PAUL'S HEAD

APPENDIX 1: TABLE OF CATEGORIES

Entry	God	Being	Entity	Place
Ancient of Days (1)	x			
Angel (2)		x		
Angel of the Lord (3)		x		
Ancient Path (4)				x
Apostle (Office) (5)		x		
Archangel (5a)		x		
Armor of Light (6)	x			
Authorities (7)		x		
Authority (8)		x		
Book (9)			x	
Branch (10)			x	
Breakthrough Angel, Breakthrough Anointing (11)		x		
Bronze Man (12)		x		
Burning Bush (25)	x		x	
Candlestick (74)			x	
Captain/Commander of the Host (13)		x		
Certain Holy One (69)		x		
Chariots of Fire (14)		x		
Cherub(im) (15)		x		
Chromosome (16)			x	
Cloud (17)			x	
Cloud of Witnesses (18)				x
Council of the Lord (19)				x
Deep (20)			x	x
Depth (21)			x	x
Dominion (34)		x		
Door/Gate (22)			x	
Elder (23)		x		
Elemental Spirit (24)			x	

	God	Being	Entity	Place
Encouragement (28)		x		
Eternity/Burning Bush/I AM (25)	x			
Evangelist (Office) (26)		x		
Exhortation (28)		x		
Father as Power (29)	x			
Femaleness (30)	x	x	x	x
Fiery Stones (31)			x	
Furnace (32)		x		
Gabriel (33)		x		
Dominion/Grid/Wall (22)			x	
Gatekeeper/Doorkeeper (35)		x		
Giving (36)		x		
Glorious Ones (37)		x		
Glory of God (38)	x			
Golden Bowl (39)			x	
Golden Pipes (40)		x		
Glory Realm (41)	x			
Grid (82)				x
Healing (42)		x		x
Height (43)		x		x
Highways of Holiness (44)			x	
Holiness (45)		x		
Holy Spirit (46)	x			
Honey (47)			x	
Horns (38)		x		
Horse (48)		x		
Host (49)		x		
I AM (25)	x			
JEHOVAH JIREH (50)	x			
Kairos (51)		x		
Law (52)		x		
Leader (53)		x		

	God	Being	Entity	Place
Length (54)			x	x
Ley Lines			x	
Library (55)			x	x
Lightnings (56)			x	
Lion of Judah (27)	x			
Little Scroll (57)			x	
Living Word (58)			x	
Majesty (59)			x	x
Maleness (60)	x	x	x	x
Marriage (61)			x	
Mazzaroth (62)		x		
Michael (63)		x		
Melchizedek (64)	x			
Mercy (65)		x		
Morning Star (93)		x		
Mt. Zion (66)			x	x
Olive Trees (67)		x		
Order of Melchizedek (68)	x			x
Certain Holy One/Palmoni (69)		x		
Pastor (Office) (70)		x		
Path(way) (71)			x	
Pillar (72)		x		
Pillar of Fire (3)		x		
Pool of Bethesda (73)			x	
Power/Candlestick (74)		x		
Powers of Age to Come (74)	x			
Prophet (Office) (75)		x		
Prophet (Spiritual Gift) (76)		x		
Radiant Glory (6)	x			
Rainbow Angel (77)		x		
Refiner's Fire (78)		x		
Refuge (79)		x		

	God	Being	Entity	Place
River of God (25)			x	x
Roots (80)			x	
Ruler (81)		x		
Scribe (83)		x		
Scroll (9)			x	
Selah (84)		x		
Seraphim (85)		x		
Seven Eyes of the Lord (See Appendix 4)		x		x
Seven Spirits of God (86)		x		x
Seven Thunders (87)		x		
Shield of Faith (88)			x	
Silver Cord (89)			x	
Son of Man (90)	x			
son(s) of God (91)		x		
Spiritual Forces (92)		x		
Star (93)		x		
Sun of Righteousness (94)		x		
Teacher (Office) (95)		x		
Teacher (Spiritual Gift) (96)		x		
Throne (97)		x		
Thummin (101)			x	
Tongues of Man (98)		x		
Tongues of Angels (99)		x		
Tree of Life (74)		x		
Truth (100)		x		
Urim and Thummin (101)			x	
Voice of Many Waters (102)	x			
Walls (34)			x	x
Watcher (103)		x		
Whirlwind (104)			x	
Width (105)			x	x
Window (106)			x	

	God	Being	Entity	Place
Wisdom (107)		x		
Womb of the Dawn (108)			x	x
Word of Life (109)	x			
Zodiac ((62)		x		

APPENDIX 2: DISCERNMENT OBSERVATIONS

EVIL:

1. Any discernment of evil might be experienced in the same manner as something that is righteous, the difference being that the 'evil default' discernment happens simultaneously. For example, if a power is discerned concurrently with evil, then it would be a fallen power rather than a righteous one.

2. Sometimes evil (i.e. witchcraft) may be felt as nausea, sleepiness, inability to focus. Or, it may be smelled as a terribly unpleasant odor.

3. Gossip is felt like spider webs on the feet (Paul); on the chin or lower jaw (Rob); feels sharp pains in the back in regard to the person targeted and also as well spider webs around the feet (Jana)

4. Paul feels pain in the supra-pubic area when discerning Jezebel

DISCERNING BY FEELING WITH THE HANDS:

1. Sometimes objects manifest and need to be discerned. These could include such things as swords, scrolls/books, vases of oil, scepters, mantles, rods, etc. We may know something is there through a word of knowledge or partial discernment, such as feeling like something weighty has been placed in one's hands. Or something may be seen, such as a gate, but not clearly. In these cases we feel around with our hands, kind of like a blind person or someone grouping around in the dark to figure out what something is.

2. Beings/entities/places may also be discerned by feeling at times.

   a. For example, an angel may manifest and by moving one's hand into where it is known to be, specific bodily sensation can be identified.

   b. This technique is very helpful when learning how to discern because when the hand is 'in the angel' the manner of discernment may be sensed in the body in another manner as well as/instead of a feeling on the hand.

    c. Sometimes the location is felt as a slight pressure or heaviness in the air, or as a tingling in the hands.

3. Discerning with senses other than touch require practice as one learns to understand what each sensation indicates:

    a. Hearing—such things as stars, saints singing, angels speaking in tongues, shifting on the grid, and musical note or tones produce common sounds

    b. Seeing—visions of various kinds, dreams

    c. Smell—people often report various smells that indicate both righteous and unrighteous thing. Common smells include such aromas as flowers, perfume, incense, smoke, fresh bread, etc. Evil smells: sulfur, cigarette smoke; poverty like garbage; demonic like something dead

    d. Taste—may taste a specific food or flavor; may be sour, sweet, bitter, etc.

APPENDIX 3: SEVEN EYES OF THE LORD

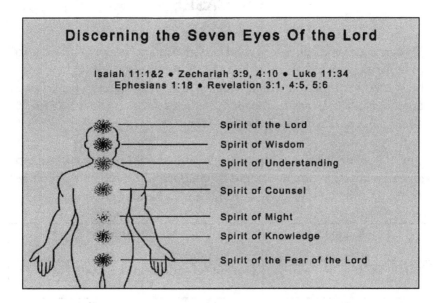

Discerning the Seven Eyes Of the Lord

Isaiah 11:1&2 • Zechariah 3:9, 4:10 • Luke 11:34
Ephesians 1:18 • Revelation 3:1, 4:5, 5:6

- Spirit of the Lord
- Spirit of Wisdom
- Spirit of Understanding
- Spirit of Counsel
- Spirit of Might
- Spirit of Knowledge
- Spirit of the Fear of the Lord

If this were in color, the seven eyes would be indicated by the colors of the rainbow:

- Violet   Spirit of the LORD
- Indigo   Spirit of Wisdom
- Blue   Spirit of Understanding
- Green   Spirit of Counsel
- Yellow   Spirit of Might
- Orange   Spirit of Knowledge
- Red   Spirit of the Fear of the LORD

APPENDIX 4: DISCERNMENT OF DISEASES

Discernment is often a tool the Lord gives us to understand how to pray for healing in others. When the discernment occurs, there may be someone in the immediate vicinity that God wants to heal. For a thorough discussion of healing miracles, see *Exploring Heavenly Places, Volume 6: Miracles on the Mountain of the Lord*

The following list is a sampling only, and should not be considered an exhaustive list, but is offered to encourage the reader to become aware of and begin using discernment with healing prayer.

Disease	Discernment
Ankle Injury	Painful sensation on the ankle
Asthma	Sensation just below the collarbone
Arthritis, Tendonitis, Bursitis, Etc.	Painful sensation in the elbow
Back Problems	Sensation in the back/spine
Breast Cancer	Sensation across breast or heart
Collarbone Problems	Sensation on the collarbone (Note: the clavicle can also refer to unity)
Diabetes	Felt over the pancreas, which is mid-left side of stomach
Eye Issues	A sensation over one or both eyes
Female Problems	Sensation across pubic bone

Glandular Issues (Pituitary, Thyroid, Etc.)	Sensation on the front of the neck
Groin Issues	Sensation over the groin area (Note: may also indicate a spirit of sexual abuse, Jezebel, female goddess etc.)
Hemorrhoids	Sensation in the rectum
Heart Disease	Sensation over the heart
Heel Problems	Sensation on your heel; and if the Achilles, a sensation on the Achilles
Inner Ear Problems (Vertigo, Infection, Tinnitus, Etc.)	Piercing of flashing pain deep in the ear
Orthopedic problems (Hip, Jaw, Knee, Neck, Ribs, Etc.)	Sensation on the affected part of the body
Pancreas	Sensation on the left side of the back
Throat problem (Infection, Cancer, Etc.)	Sensation in the throat
Skin Disorders (Eczema, Hives, Psoriasis, Etc.)	Itchy sensation on affected area(s)